# Celtic

## Art

In Britain before
the Roman Conquest

*Ian Stead*

THE BRITISH MUSEUM PRESS

First published 1985
Second edition 1996
Reprinted 2003

A catalogue record for this
book is available from the
British Library

ISBN 0-7141-2117-7

Designed by Carroll Associates
Typeset in Van Dijck®
Cover design by Martin Richards
Printed in China by Imago

Jacket illustration *The central
panel of the Battersea shield,
raised in repoussé and with red
'enamel' decoration.*

Right *Bronze boar figurines:
the three on the left are from
Hounslow and the other (height
32 mm) is from Camerton.*

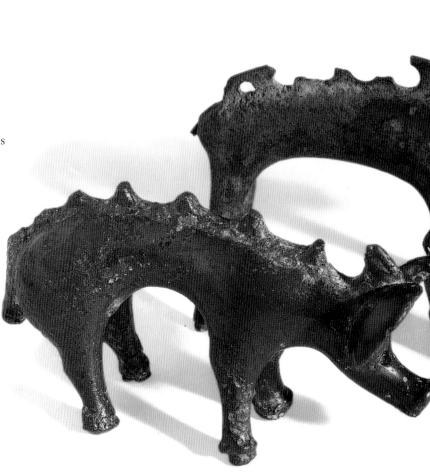

# Contents

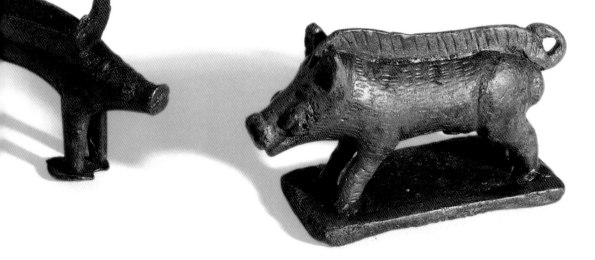

# Introduction

THIS BOOK is concerned with the British Iron Age, the five hundred years or so before the birth of Christ, when England, Wales and part of Scotland were inhabited by the Celtic-speaking Britons. Their language, British, was spoken but never written, so it is hardly surprising that their written history is brief, comprising a few references in Greek and Latin mainly by writers who knew very little about those remote islands at the edge of the world. But three Latin writers did visit Britain, and the earliest and most important was Julius Caesar, who organised military expeditions here in 55 and 54 BC. Before Caesar history has little to say about Britain, and not a single Briton is known by name. A little can be gleaned from accounts of their relatives, the Gauls, where one of the most important sources is Posidonius (135-51 BC), a Greek ethnographer whose lost work was used in the first century BC by Diodorus Siculus, Strabo and even Caesar. But most information about the Britons has to come from the discipline of the prehistorian. By the study of artefacts, excavation, field-work and aerial photography masses of facts can be accumulated about certain aspects of their life; but in the

1 *Air photograph of the settlement at Gussage All Saints in the course of excavation. Ditches define the settlement (c.100 x 120 m) and some of the buildings; the other prominent features are pits, one of which produced an important collection of metal-working debris.*

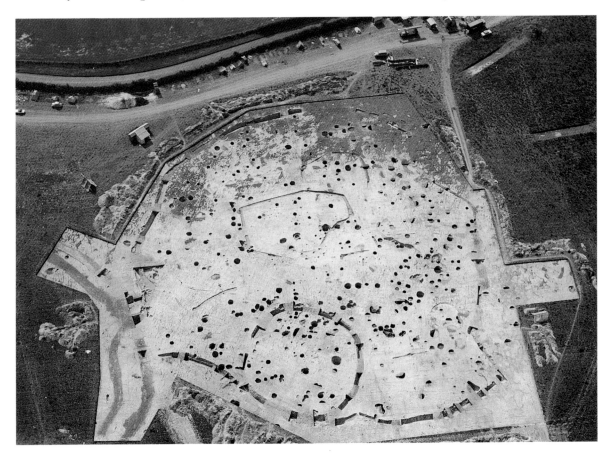

absence of the written word much about the Britons will never be known.

Without chronicles a time-scale has to be constructed, and this is a laborious process bedevilled by uncertainties. Modern techniques are of little help: Carbon-14 dating, for instance, which is vital for the earlier stages of prehistory, is of little use for this period. The date of one very important deposit in a pit excavated at Gussage All Saints (Dorset) [1] is estimated by radio carbon analysis to be between 355 and 20 BC, but the chances of the true date falling within these limits is only 68 per cent. The margin of error is huge, and such dates are in any case only rarely associated with significant artefacts. Dendrochronology, the counting of tree-rings, is a far more exact technique: it has shown, for instance, that a wooden shield found near the edge of Lake Neuchâtel in Switzerland was shaped from a tree felled in 229 BC. But well-preserved wood survives only in exceptional circumstances. For the material in this book chronology is derived from artefacts - their typology and associations.

The first attempts to construct a chronology for European prehistory were made in the nineteenth century and were based on the materials used for basic tools: three Ages were defined, of Stone, Bronze and Iron. The latest, the Iron Age, was subdivided in 1872 into two periods named after important assemblages recently unearthed. The first took its name from a huge cemetery near the salt mines at Hallstatt in Upper Austria, and the second was called La Tène after a site on the shores of Lake Neuchâtel, where an impressive collection of objects had been found when the water-levels of the Swiss lakes were re-aligned. The two names are applied because, in a very general way, those sites produced artefacts typical of their respective periods: they are no more than type-sites, and there is no suggestion that the cultures they represent originated at those sites, still less that those names would have meant anything at all to the peoples thus labelled by archaeologists.

The La Tène period, which is the main concern of this book, was subdivided into Early, Middle and Late as long ago as 1885 on the basis of the typologies of brooches, swords and scabbards, which throughout Celtic Europe developed along roughly similar lines. At the turn of the century two parallel classifications were established: La Tène I-III in France, and La Tène A-D in Germany. With various sub-divisions these two systems still operate today. But relative chronology is not an end in itself: it provides a framework to which absolute dates must be attached. Although dendrochronology is already of some help here, it has yet to supersede traditional approaches which rely on dates given by contacts with the literate civilisations of Greece and Italy. Greek and Latin histories, the occasional discovery of Greek and Italian objects in Celtic graves, and even the odd Celtic object in a classical context enable absolute dates to be applied to Celtic antiquities. The resulting chronology for the La Tène period can be stated only in the most general of terms: La Tène I (450-250 BC), II (250-100 BC) and III (100 BC to the Roman conquest).

Over the centuries Iron Age artefacts must have been found and discarded wherever the ground was tilled or otherwise disturbed. By the eighteenth century, with the industrial and agricultural revolutions, the

2 *Short iron sword with bronze handle and bronze scabbard, found in the River Witham, but now lost. This illustration was published by Franks in* Horae Ferales *(1863). Full length said to be 380 mm.*

pace of those disturbances and consequent discoveries increased and coincided with a growing interest in history and antiquities. One of the earliest recorded Iron Age artefacts in Britain is a Celtic bronze carnyx (trumpet) - still the most complete example known - found when the River Witham in Lincolnshire was being dredged in 1768. It was acquired by Sir Joseph Banks, a local worthy and a scholar with an international reputation, who allowed a zealous scientist to destroy it in order to determine its composition. Other antiquities dredged from the Witham have also been lost, including a remarkable short sword in a bronze scabbard: the hilt is of bronze and its pommel was represented (perhaps misrepresented) as a kind of Lincoln imp [2]. In the eighteenth century some antiquities found their way into cabinets of curiosities, but in the nineteenth century collectors took to the field: in 1815 the Revd E.W. Stillingfleet 'joined a party, which was formed for the purpose of opening a group of barrows' at Arras (East Yorkshire) and came across Iron Age skeletons with some impressive grave-goods. By the middle of the century a considerable number of Iron Age antiquities were known, mainly chance finds, including some remarkable pieces dredged from the Thames and the Witham. Many were published by A.W. Franks in an outstanding contribution to *Horae Ferales* (1863) [2, 3, 5]: Franks saw the British antiquities in a European context, and was ahead of his Continental colleagues in recognising them as Celtic. From the end of the nineteenth century archaeological excavations became more sophisticated and recovered artefacts in contexts that enabled them to provide ever more information about the past. In recent years the hobby of metal detecting has produced a huge haul of artefacts, including one or two really fine pieces [4].

For every metal object that was buried, either deliberately or by chance, there must have been many more that were used until they were broken, worn or obsolete and then recycled. The surviving sample is minute. Caesar mentioned 4,000 chariots retained by the British king Cassivellaunus, and each of those chariots would have been drawn by two horses, each with a horse-bit and with shared harness using five terrets (rein-rings). Of those 8,000 horse-bits and 20,000 terrets is there a single one in our museums today? Probably not. Even the small sample now available for study may be distorted, because objects that were deliberately buried may well have been specially selected and need not be typical of the objects of the day. With pottery the problems are not so marked: pots are fragile and readily broken, but once they are buried either complete or in sherds they are well-nigh indestructible. As well as metal and pottery a vast range of organic materials such as wood, skin

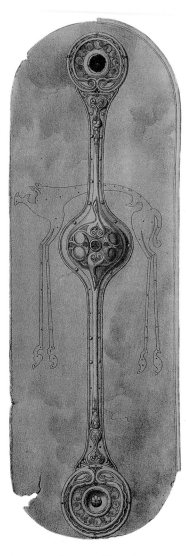

3 *The Witham shield as illustrated by Franks in* Horae Ferales *(1863). This illustration shows clearly the outlines of a boar which once decorated the shield. Length 1.13 m.*

and fabrics was much used by the Celts, as by all primitive peoples. These materials gradually deteriorate in use and only a small percentage would be buried; unless they were deposited in an exceptional environment their deterioration would then be accelerated. In our climate only water-logged conditions will preserve organic materials, and the sample available for study is negligible.

Most Celtic art takes the form of abstract decoration on functional objects, which would have appealed to the Celt because of its meaning or usefulness but which is also in tune with current taste. Sensitive and appreciative modern writers have made valiant efforts to interpret its meaning, but the imagination of modern people is an unreliable guide to the aims, beliefs and feelings of their primitive forebears. Only the Celtic artists and their patrons could explain Celtic art, and as they never set pen to paper their knowledge died with them. This book attempts to approach the subject on fairly solid ground, starting with techniques of metalwork (because most surviving examples are of metal), then following the development of certain patterns, and finally giving examples of decorated artefacts used by the Britons in various walks of life.

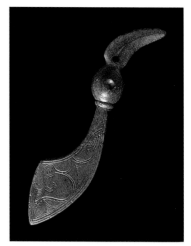

4 *A small bronze hooked blade with a fine decorated handle. The decoration is in the 'Witham-Wandsworth Style' (see p. 29), and the overall shape is comparable with motifs on the Wandsworth round-boss (fig. 80). Found by a metal detectorist at St Stephen (Herts). Length 110 mm.*

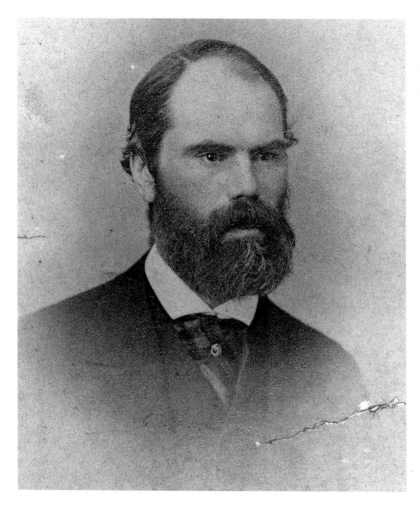

5 *Augustus Wollaston Franks (1826-97) joined the British Museum's staff in 1851, was Keeper of the Department of British and Medieval Antiquities 1866-96 and one of the Museum's greatest benefactors.*

# Chapter One | Metalworking techniques

6 *The central panel of the Battersea shield, raised in repoussé and with red 'enamel' decoration. Diameter 290 mm.*

BRONZE HAD already been worked in Britain for over a millennium before the Iron Age began but it was still of prime importance, particularly for decorative work. Most soils are gentler to bronze than to iron, and apart from a usually greenish patina much of it differs little from the day when it was lost or discarded. Bronze is an alloy of copper and tin, and judging from analyses it was carefully mixed to obtain a precise balance between the two. Copper was mined in the

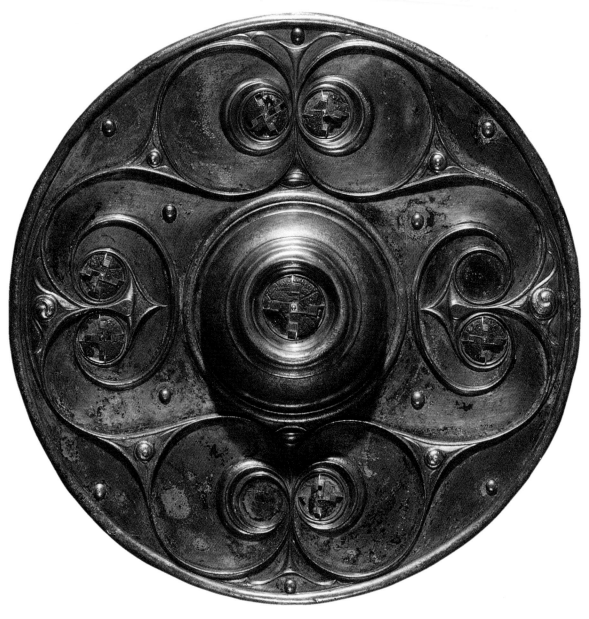

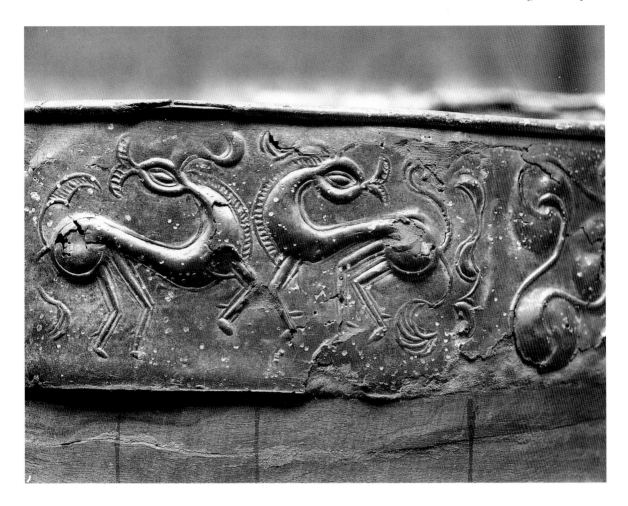

south-west of England, in Wales, Scotland and Ireland, and Cornish tin was well known in the ancient world and attracted explorers from as far afield as Greece. But foreign ores were also used in Britain, for Caesar records that bronze was imported and analyses have shown that this practice went back into the Bronze Age. Sheet bronze was made by casting an ingot and beating it into a thin sheet; then it could be cut and decorated in various ways. Some of the more ambitious products, such as the famous shield-bosses, were decorated by repoussé - raising the design by hammering from the underside, with the object presumably resting on a bed of resilient pitch [6]. Relatively small pieces were mass-produced by using a 'former' into which a master design had been cut: both iron and bronze formers are known but wood could also have been used. The sheet bronze to be decorated would then be placed over the former and beaten into the recessed shapes to create a number of identical patterns. Some of the decoration on the Aylesford bucket was made in this way: of the three designs on its upper band two occur four times and one twice - each time the impressions are identical. In at least one place, at the side of the 'pantomime horses', there is an impression of a vertical line which may well have been made by the edge of a former [7]. Relief

7 *A detail of the decoration on the Aylesford bucket (fig. 58). The two fantastic animals have been shaped in a former, and there is an identical impression on the opposite side of the bucket. The vertical edges of the former can be distinguished, especially on the right.*

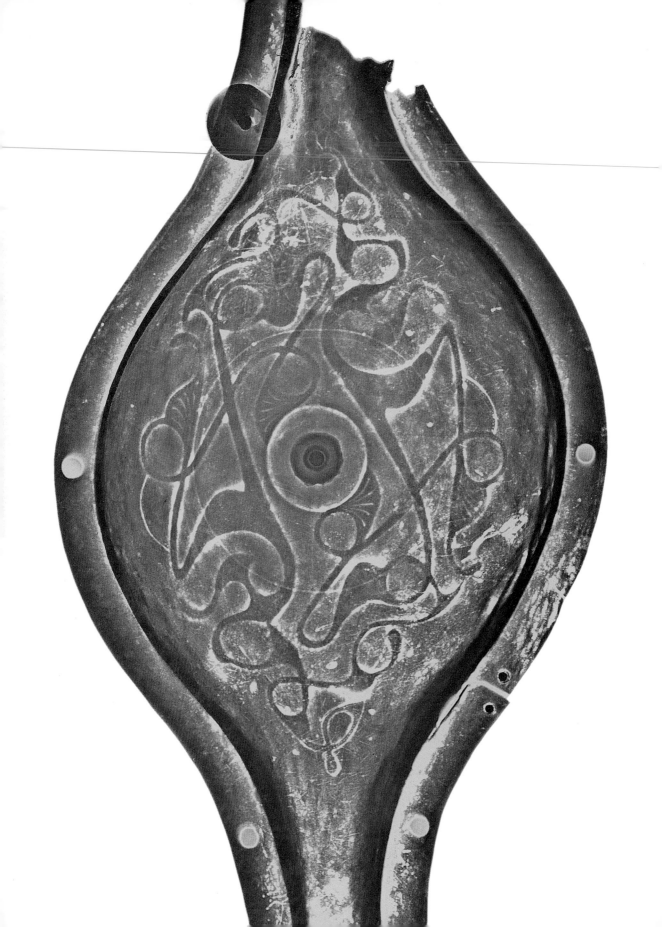

decoration was also achieved by working the surface of sheet bronze, lowering the background to leave the design standing proud. The decoration on the Ratcliffe shield-boss is an outstanding example of this rarely used technique [8].

Surface decoration was sometimes inscribed or scratched using a fine-pointed scriber to produce a sharp line. This tool was used alone in some designs, but in others it was employed for the preliminary mapping out. More pronounced lines could have been engraved with a graver, which is pushed over the surface and held in the fingers rather as one would hold a pencil; a somewhat similar effect is produced by chasing, in which a tracer is hammered forward across the metal. If the marks are well preserved it may be possible to identify the tools that made them and in some instances it has been possible to follow the development of the tool in the course of the work - such as the stages at which its edge was chipped and subsequently resharpened [9]. Unfortunately the fine tools themselves are difficult to identify. More substantial tools are easier to recognise and a collection from a grave at Whitcombe (Dorset) comprised an iron hammer-head and file as well as a chalk disc which could have served as the flywheel for a pump-drill. Iron files can sometimes be identified with the aid of radiography, and examples from Fiskerton

8 Opposite page *A photograph of a xeroradiograph of the bronze shield-boss found in the River Trent at Ratcliffe-on-Soar (Notts). The lighter colour shows where bronze has been removed to leave the design in relief. Note also the circular marking-out groove that is on the inside of the boss. Width 135 mm.*

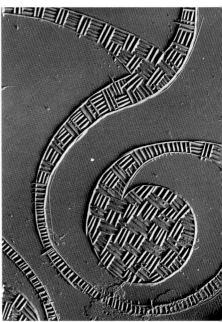

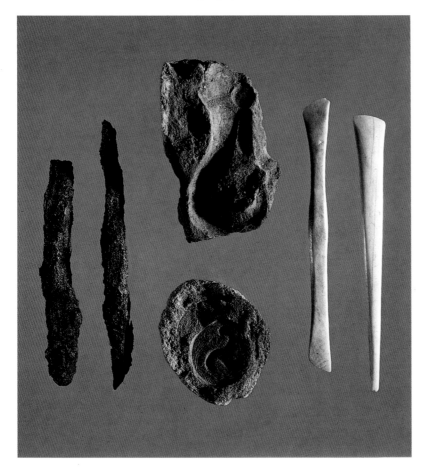

9 *Detail of a silicone rubber mould of decoration on the back of the Great Chesterford (Essex) mirror. Engraved with a common graver and a fine round-nosed graver (possibly the same tool, the edge of which was changed by resharpening); 'guide lines' are lightly scratched by a scriber.*

10 *Bone modelling tools, fired clay moulds (for a link of a horse-bit, above, and the head of a linch-pin, below) and the corroded remains of iron or steel tools. From pit 209 at Gussage All Saints. Length of bone tool (right) 82 mm.*

11 *The end of a bronze scabbard from Bugthorpe (East Yorks). The sheet bronze front-plate, decorated with a graver or tracer, is attached to an iron back-plate by the binding strips of a chape, also cut from sheet bronze. The chape-end has been cast-on to the binding strips and its decoration is part of the lost-wax casting. Width of chape-end 43 mm.*

(Lincs) and Gussage All Saints (Dorset) had specks of bronze in the grooves, showing that they had been used by bronze-workers.

Sometimes the bronze-smith tried out the effects of a tool on part of an object that would be hidden from view. On the Birdlip mirror, for instance, there are practice tool-marks in the area subsequently covered by the bronze handle. Similarly a design had been roughly worked on the inner face of a scabbard-plate found in the River Bann in Northern Ireland. Bone would have been an ideal medium on which to sketch designs intended for bronze, and a collection of bone flakes with compass-drawn ornament from Lough Crew (Co. Meath) seems to have been used in this way. Their context is curious, because they were found in a tomb which would then have been some 3,000 years old. Among the Lough Crew finds was what may well have been a pair of compasses (now lost) and it seems reasonable to interpret the collection as workshop debris. Compasses were undoubtedly used by some Celtic artists and very complex designs were constructed. Detailed study of the decoration on the back of the Holcombe (Devon) mirror has shown that it could have been formed entirely from compass arcs, and some grooves on its surface can only have been made by heavy scratching with compasses. Designs could have been laid out directly on the bronze by first coating it with a thin layer of wax and using something like a transparent slice of horn below the centre-point to ensure that it did not mark the metal surface.

Another way of producing decorative bronze-work was by lost-wax casting. The object was first modelled in wax, and sometimes elaborately decorated at this stage. Then the mould was made by encasing the object in clay, heating to melt and remove the wax, and firing to harden the clay. Bronze of a slightly different alloy from sheet bronze (lead was added to increase the fluidity), poured into the clay mould, would take on the exact form of the modelled wax. The fired clay would have to be broken open so the mould could never be used again. Finally the bronze object was finished by filing, polishing and perhaps by the addition of more detail using the tools already described for decorating sheet bronze. This method of production must have created a huge quantity of broken moulds, but very few have been recognised. The best collection was discovered in pit 209 on the settlement at Gussage All Saints (Dorset) (see fig. 1) where more than 7,000 fragments of moulds had been discarded [10]. The Gussage bronze-smith made harness and chariot fittings, and he would have had a workshop on the site but nothing of it survived: it is known only because some of the debris was swept up and dumped in a pit. Among the rubbish were some of the tools used for modelling the wax. Ironically these fragile bone implements are still in perfect condition, whereas the hard steel tools used by the same craftsman have been reduced to virtually unrecognisable lengths of corrosion products.

Cast bronze was used to make some complete objects, but it was also a component of more complex objects. Sword scabbards were sometimes made of bronze: two scabbard-plates would be cut from the sheet, one wrapped round the edges of the other, and their lower parts secured by a sheet bronze chape [11]. But the very end of the chape was usually cast-on to the frame. The bronze-smith must have worked in close co-operation with the blacksmith - sometimes perhaps the same craftsman carried out both trades in the same workshop. Pit 209 at Gussage All Saints included scale produced by forging iron as well as moulds for casting bronze. Bronze was cast-on to iron to make vehicle fittings and harness [12], and sometimes iron was covered with bronze, either dipped in molten bronze or, as with the rings of many horse-bits, encased in sheet bronze.

12 *A pair of linch-pins with iron shanks and cast bronze terminals, from a cart-burial at Kirkburn (East Yorks). Length 120 mm.*

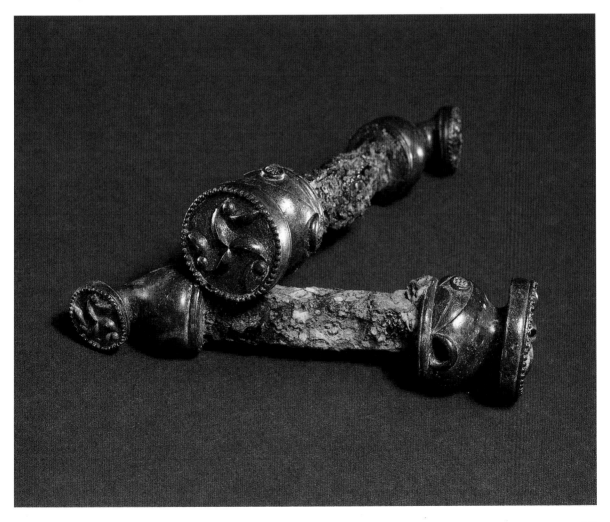

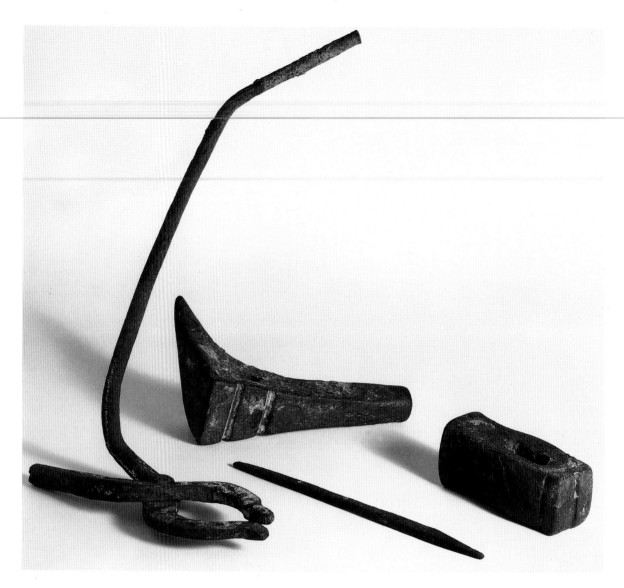

13 *Some of the blacksmiths' tools from the Waltham Abbey hoard: tongs, anvil, head of a sledge-hammer and file. The anvil and the head of the sledge-hammer have been grooved so that they could be used as swages. The file is 232 mm long.*

14 Opposite page *Head of an iron fire-dog found at Baldock; the complete fire-dog is 700 mm high.*

Iron was first worked in Britain in the seventh century BC. More widespread and plentiful, and therefore cheaper, iron ores were usually obtained from shallow opencast workings in close proximity to the woodland needed to provide charcoal for smelting. One of the earliest iron-producing sites in Britain might well have been at Brooklands, near Weybridge (Surrey), where a well-known deposit of iron ore was still being worked in the nineteenth century. The date of the Iron Age workings at Brooklands is difficult to establish because the only associated artefacts are imprecisely dated, but it is tempting to link them with a Hallstatt C bronze bucket found only 100 m away. Remains of iron-smelting furnaces excavated at Brooklands are no more than a simple bowl which would have been surmounted by a fired clay shaft: there was no provision for tapping the slag which would have collected in the bottom, so that the furnace had to be dismantled to remove both bloom and

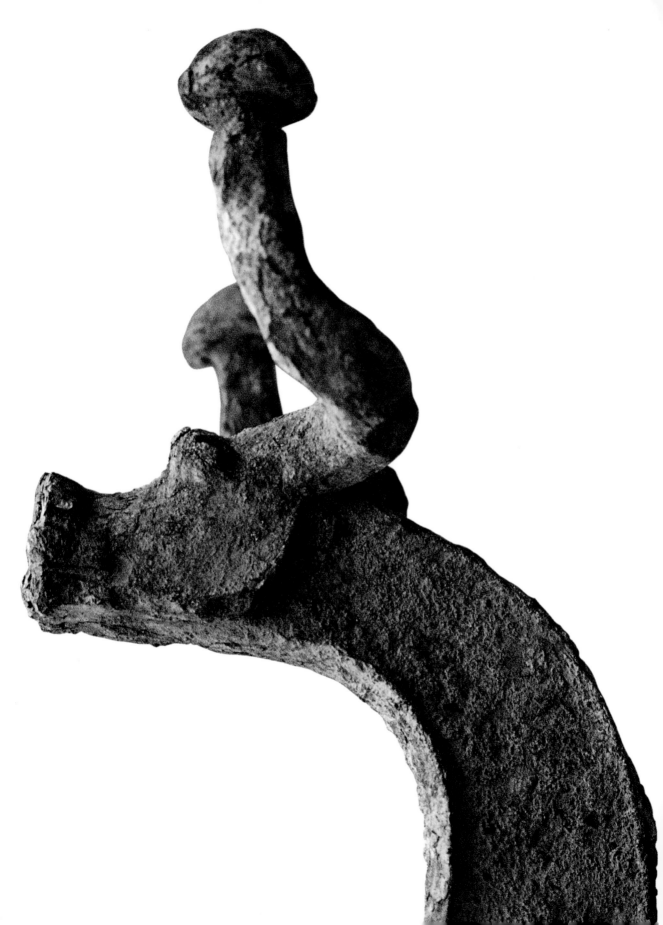

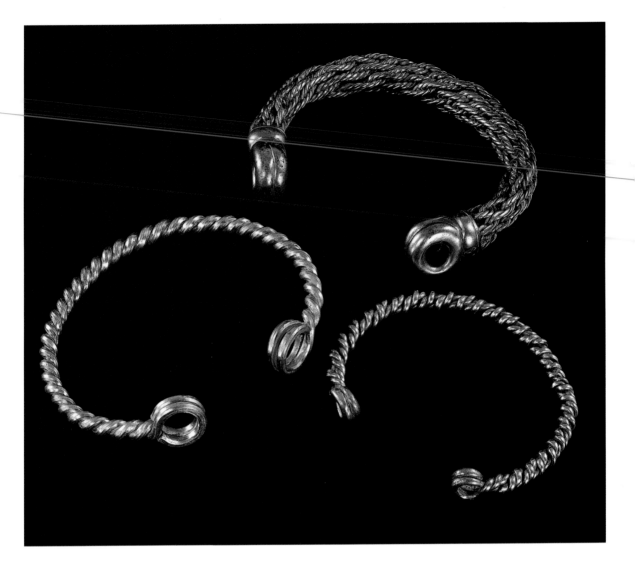

15 *Three silver torques from a hoard found at Snettisham in 1990. The torque on the left measures 185 mm across externally.*

16 Opposite page *The central boss of the Witham shield (see fig. 3).*

slag. Iron could not be worked in the same way as bronze; for instance, it does not melt at the temperatures achieved in the Iron Age. Instead, the smelted bloom was forged, which means that the iron was repeatedly brought to a red heat and hammered to produce the finished object. Both smelting and forging were carried out at Brooklands.

The Iron Age blacksmith seems to have had most of the skills and most of the tools used by village blacksmiths until recent times. His hallmark is the long-handled tongs needed to hold the red-hot iron at a comfortable distance. A small hoard of ironwork from Waltham Abbey (Essex) included the tools of a blacksmith; those that could be broken had been deliberately smashed, presumably as part of a ritual, before the hoard was deposited in the River Lea. As well as five pairs of tongs, the blacksmith's tools included three small anvils, the head of a sledge-hammer, a file and a poker, in a collection dating from the first century BC or AD [13]. Two of the anvils could be reversed for use as mandrels (over

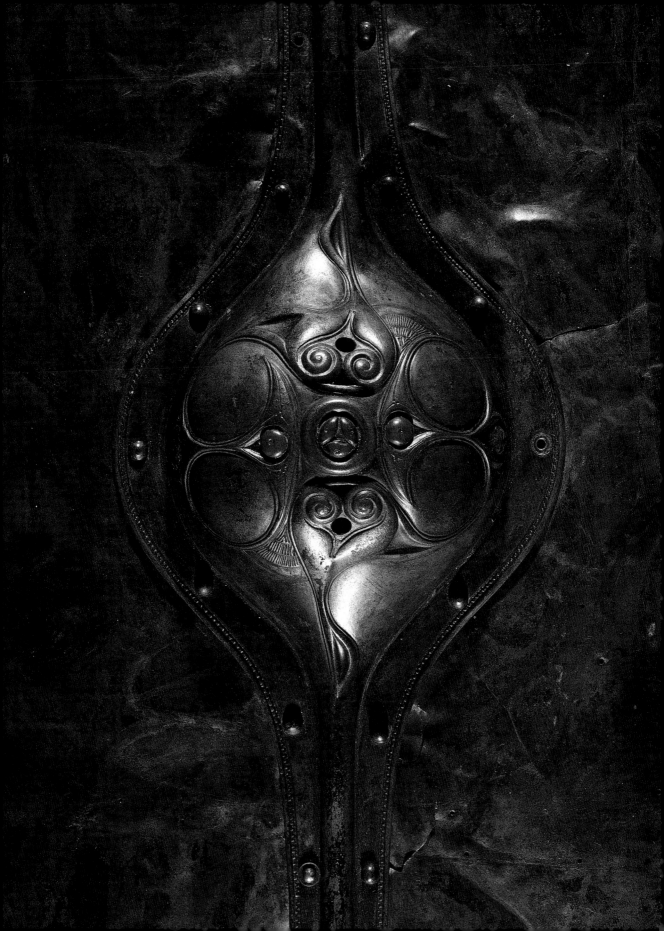

which bars and rods could be bent) and were also grooved for rounding metal rods. The rods would be shaped between an upper and a lower groove, or swage: in the Waltham Abbey collection the anvils served as the lower swages and the head of the sledge-hammer had been grooved to double as an upper swage. Multi-purpose tools like these suggest that the blacksmith was itinerant because he seems to have been anxious to keep the number of heavy tools to a minimum. Ancient tools are by no means common because they would have been highly prized and passed from one generation to another, and when worn out they would have been recycled. Unassociated iron tools are difficult to date because the same forms remain in use for centuries, so most blacksmiths' tools of the Iron Age are known only from deliberate deposits in hoards or graves. The Iron Age blacksmith also had hammers, set-hammers, hot-chisels, and slices (a long poker-like tool with a spatulate end used for controlling the hot fuel).

One of the finest products of the Iron Age blacksmith is the fire-dog, and the head from one found at Baldock (Herts) is an especially impressive piece of work [14]. The tall upright has been bent outwards at the top to form the basis of the head, from which the snout has been forged, the nostrils punched and the mouth and prominent jaw-line chiselled. The horns would have been forged separately, welded on top of the head, and their ends shaped into protruding eyes. Iron could also be engraved or chased, provided the graver or tracer was hard enough, but surface corrosion has left us few good examples.

Of other metals silver, listed by Strabo as a British export, was sometimes alloyed with gold but was rarely used as a predominant metal. The most ancient silver artefact from Britain is a finger-ring from Park Brow (Sussex) belonging to a distinctive type found mainly in Switzerland and dating from the third century BC. Otherwise until recently the earliest silver objects from the British Iron Age were coins and a few brooches dating from the second half of the first century BC. But in 1990 the picture was transformed when five hoards of torques buried about 70 BC were found at Snettisham (Norfolk): they contained 11 kilos of silver and a similar quantity of gold [15]. Silver occurs naturally as an alloy of gold, and when it is a significant component the alloy is known as electrum, but at Snettisham some torques were relatively pure, with alloys including up to 89 per cent silver.

Gold was used much more frequently than silver, and had a much longer history: the earliest gold artefacts in Britain date back to the second millennium BC. Always valuable, gold objects suffered especially from recycling and many a work of art must have been consigned to the crucible to produce Britain's gold coinage. Alone among the metals, gold does not corrode and comes out of the ground as bright as when it was last seen in the Iron Age. Although they would have worked it in the same way as bronze, the Britons hardly ever used gold for brooches, and only very rarely for bracelets, but gold torques feature prominently among British antiquities.

In the first century BC British metalworkers experimented with means of making base metals appear more valuable. Bronze was some-

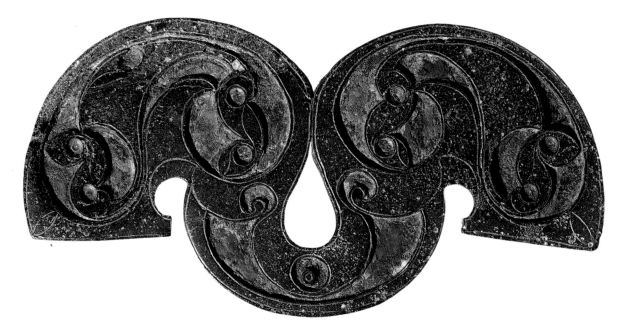

times plated with silver-copper alloy to give it the appearance of silver, and sometimes gilded by coating it with an amalgam of gold and mercury and then heating to drive off excess mercury.

Metalwork, especially bronze, was occasionally enhanced by the addition of coloured ornaments. Precious coral from the Mediterranean was applied in the form of knobs or strips to a variety of objects, often attached by bronze pins or rivets. Some brooches from the Yorkshire graves have huge amounts of coral, the colour of which has been reduced from pink to white as a result of centuries in the earth (see fig. 40). The Witham shield has knobs of coral that still retain their original, very deep, colour [16]. On the Continent coral is rarely used after La Tène I, but in Britain it continued into La Tène III: indeed coral in the Polden Hills (Somerset) hoard shows that it was still employed at the time of the Roman conquest. Shell, amber and stone ornaments are also known, but the most common alternative to coral was red glass or 'enamel'. The glass usually has an opaque 'sealing-wax red' colour which is given by crystals of cuprous oxide. It was used in small lumps which could be softened by heating and then shaped into small pellets to be attached by bronze pins; secured onto roughly keyed surfaces; or held by cut-out bronze frames (see fig. 6). By the first century AD champlevé enamel was made in some quantity: with this technique a slightly sunken field is prepared either in the original casting or by subsequent cutting, and the enamel is applied as a powder and fused in an oven. The effect is to produce a flat field of enamel whose surface is flush with that of the surrounding metal [17]. Britain was famous for its enamel-work, as Philostratus recorded early in the third century AD: 'they say that the barbarians who live in the Ocean pour [these] colours on to heated bronze and that they adhere, and grow hard as stone, keeping the designs that are made in them'.

17 *Bronze harness-fitting decorated with red champlevé enamel, from the Polden Hills hoard. Length 151 mm.*

# Chapter Two | Art styles

INSULAR CELTIC (or La Tène) art must be studied in a European context, for in the early stages Britain is an outlying province of the Continental tradition. But from the third century BC British art receives a new impetus, takes its own original direction, and its masterpieces outclass the products of Continental workshops. La Tène art was first classified by Paul Jacobsthal [18], a distinguished classical archaeologist who left Nazi Germany in the 1930s and settled in England. He published a detailed study of Continental Celtic art in 1944, but he never completed his work on the British material. On the Continent he recognised three styles: an 'Early Style' strongly influenced by Greek art but with some 'Oriental' and native traits; followed by the 'Waldalgesheim Style', named after a rich grave in the Rhineland; and then two contemporary sub-styles - the 'Sword Style' (though decorat-

18 *Paul Ferdinand Jacobsthal (1880-1957), Professor of Classical Archaeology at Marburg University 1912-35.*

19 Opposite page *Bronze chape on a sheath from Wandsworth, a lost-wax casting featuring concentric circles. Length of chape 66 mm.*

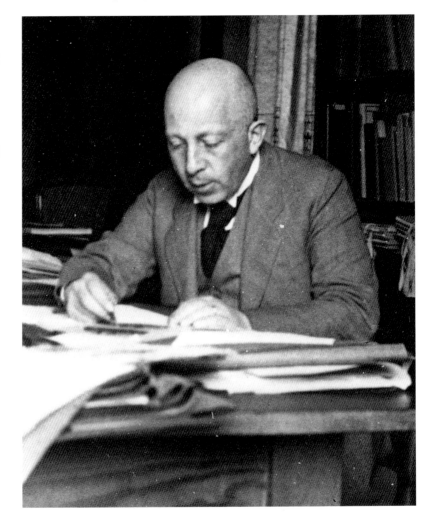

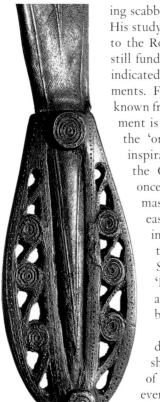

ing scabbards and not swords) and the 'Plastic Style'. His study ended within La Tène II and did not extend to the Roman conquest. Jacobsthal's classification is still fundamental, although subsequent scholars have indicated its imperfections and suggested improvements. For the 'Early Style' more material is now known from Eastern Europe, the geometric native element is more pronounced, and the precise source of the 'orientalising' influence is unclear (its main inspiration might well have been the imagination of the Celtic artist). The 'Waldalgesheim Style', once seen as the creation of a Waldalgesheim master, flows readily from the Early Style of eastern France, though there may be further influence from Italy. Many more examples of the Sword Style are now known, a 'Swiss Sword Style' has been distinguished from the 'Hungarian Sword Style', and there has been an increase in the number of decorated scabbards from France.

British Celtic art was classified by J.M. de Navarro, a Cambridge archaeologist, in a short paper that started life as one of a series of popular lectures before being broadcast and eventually published. Jacobsthal's three styles were numbered and de Navarro added a Style IV to cover British masterpieces of the third century BC. Apparently Jacobsthal disapproved of this simplification, but it does have the merit of providing a framework to guide the general reader through the complexities of La Tène art. A classification related to the Continental scheme but at the same time distinct from it is ideal because even in the early stages the British material seems to have been homemade, and in the second and first centuries BC it is only remotely linked to Continental developments. The numbered sequence has the merit of clarity, and recent research confirms its validity as a relative chronology, but the use of the word 'style' creates problems: it would be more accurate to label the development in Stages rather than Styles.

Stage I, Jacobsthal's 'Early Style', is represented by geometric Hallstatt elements and designs ultimately derived from Greek art, but there are none of the Continental 'orientalising' human masks and animal figures. The Hallstatt designs are extremely simple, such as strings of cross-hatched triangles, lozenges and compass-drawn arcs and dots, engraved or chased on bronze or iron artefacts dating from the fourth century and the end of the fifth century BC. The most complex of the geometric designs is no more than a series of circles linked by diagonal lines [19]. The more elaborate Continental Early Style art relies heavily on Greek motifs that were not slavishly copied, but adapted, dissected, and rearranged in distinctive ways. In the Rhineland disjointed elements from classical floral designs were arranged in distinctive repetitive

*20 The palmette. Celtic artists borrowed an Etruscan decorative motif, a palmette and lotus flowers, and created their own versions of the palmette, often flanked by lotus petals and arranged in a frieze: a) an Etruscan palmette and lotus flowers; b) a Celtic palmette and lotus petals on an imported Etruscan flagon now in the museum at Besançon, France; c-e: similar Celtic motifs on c) a bronze disc from Ecury-sur-Coole (Marne, France); d) a pottery jar from St Pol-de-Léon (Finistère, France); and e) the flange of a bronze helmet from Cerrig-y-Drudion (see fig. 21).*

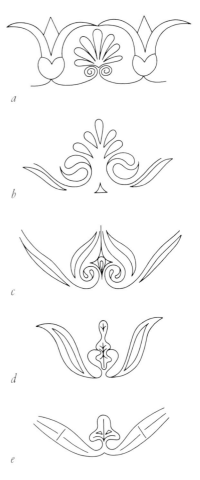

*a*

*b*

*c*

*d*

*e*

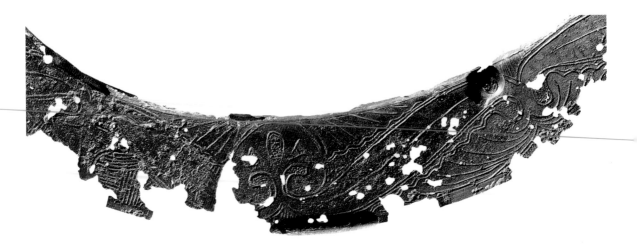

21 *Part of the decoration on the flange of a bronze helmet from Cerrig-y-Drudion (see also fig. 20): a version of the palmette flanked by lotus petals. Width of flange 28 mm.*

patterns, but in eastern France similar motifs were linked to form continuous flowing designs that influenced British Celtic art. A design based on a floral frieze of palmettes flanked by lotus flowers was especially popular [20], with elaborate variations engraved on helmets, harness and even on an imported Etruscan flagon, objects that have survived because they were deliberately buried, in graves. In Brittany similar motifs were used on pots. Work in this style is represented in Britain, and it may have been widespread, but only a little early metalwork survives because graves of the period are rare and this form of ornament was never used on British pottery. One of the few burials with metal grave-goods, found in a stone cist at Cerrig-y-Drudion (Clwyd), had been robbed and excavation in 1924 revealed only broken fragments of bronze. However, some of the fragments were from a decorated flange and sufficient survived to piece together half of a design that features palmettes and 'lotus petals' [21]. It was once thought that the flange was from a hanging-bowl, but this has now been disproved and it seems more likely to have been from a helmet. There is another version of this design on cast bronze finials from a remarkable sword-handle found by a metal detectorist at Fiskerton (Lincs), on the banks of the River Witham [22]. A third British artefact with Stage I palmettes, part of a scabbard whose bronze front-plate has a series of small crude palmettes flanked by large S-shapes [23], was acquired more than 150 years ago by 'Philosopher' Smith of Wisbech (Cambs) and presumed to be of local origin.

The principal motif of Stage II (the 'Waldalgesheim Style') is influenced by the wave tendril in Greek art and takes the form of a string of triangular shapes each linked at two corners and with a tendril sprouting from the third. Simple friezes of this type decorate elongated fields, such as sword scabbards and the bows of brooches. There are typical examples in northern Italy, where the Celts came into close contact with classical influences after their invasion early in the fourth century BC, but others are found throughout Celtic lands from Hungary to England [24]. One of the finest examples, bordering the spine of a shield from Ratcliffe-on-Soar (Notts), is very similar to one from Moscano di Fabriano (Italy), and is

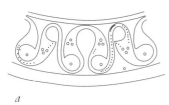

*a*

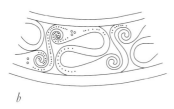

*b*

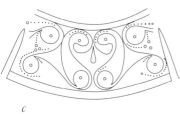

*c*

22 *The handle of a sword found at Fiskerton. Fitted with five cast bronze finials ornamented with three designs derived from Greek motifs (a - c). The handle would have been about 160 mm long.*

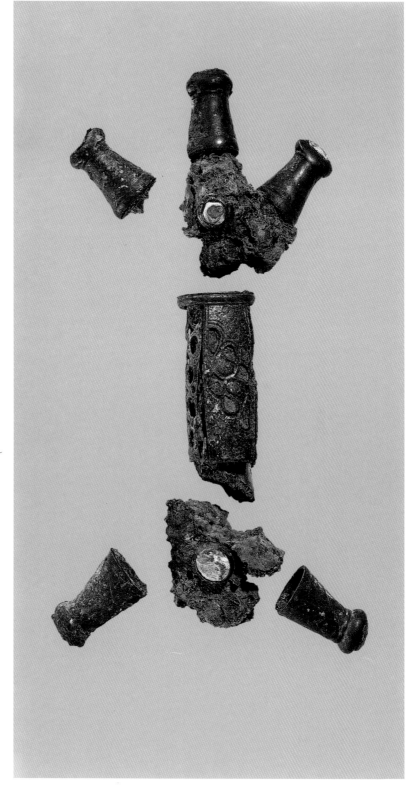

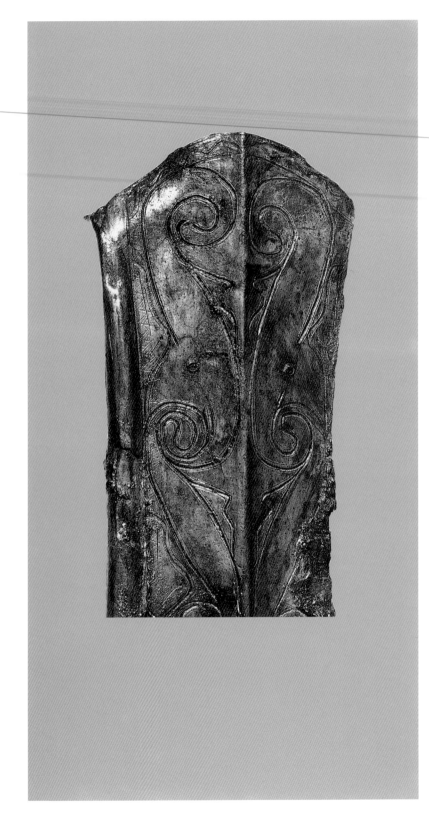

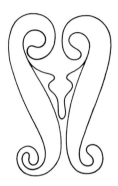

23 Upper part of a bronze
scabbard-plate from Wisbech with
a palmette (cf., figs 20d and e)
flanked by lotus petals or lyres.
Hatched triangles down the sides
are in the Hallstatt tradition.
Width 48 mm.

comparable with Continental work of the highest quality. Another frieze of the same type is on the antler handle of an iron rasp found with other tools and weapons on an archaeological excavation at Fiskerton (Lincs), the site where the Stage I sword-handle was found. But the Fiskerton example, crudely executed in pointillé, is muddled and very inferior. There are slightly different Waldalgesheim tendrils on a heavy cast bronze bracelet from a grave at Newnham Croft (Cambs), where the ornament is in a band wrapped at an angle round the body of the bracelet. Such angled banded ornament can be matched on the Continent, especially on sword scabbards. The Newnham Croft bracelet is very worn, but some hatching survives and there are hints that the entire background was so treated. This version of the design is also close to Continental models, such as the scabbard from Litér, Hungary, and there is a rather similar rendering on the scabbard found in the River Thames at Standlake (Oxon). The scabbard must have been made of wood or leather, but only two decorative bronze panels survive. The panel at the foot of the scabbard, within the chape, has the Waldalgesheim Style tendril, while the mouth is decorated with a repoussé pelta-like motif framed by a similar tendril. Both panels have hatched backgrounds, a feature much more common on British than on Continental work. The Standlake scabbard, which has a typical La Tène I chape-end and houses a La Tène I sword, dates from the end of the fourth century or the start of the third century BC. Sometimes Waldalgesheim Style triangles and tendrils flow from earlier motifs without any sharp break. They rise from the sides of palmettes on the 'Early Style' works of eastern France, on the Canosa helmet and Filottrano scabbard from Italy, on the torque from the Waldalgesheim, and on the Fiskerton sword-handle. Another example from England, from the Thames at Brentford (Greater London), is the design of three linked palmettes on a cast bronze 'horn-cap', a distinctively British artefact not found on the Continent [25].

24 *Waldalgesheim Style wave tendrils on Continental and British artefacts: a) scabbard, Moscano di Fabriano (Italy); b) shield-boss, Ratcliffe-on-Soar (Notts); c) handle of a rasp, Fiskerton (Lincs); d) scabbard, Litér (Hungary); e) bracelet, Newnham Croft (Cambs); f) scabbard, Standlake (Oxon).*

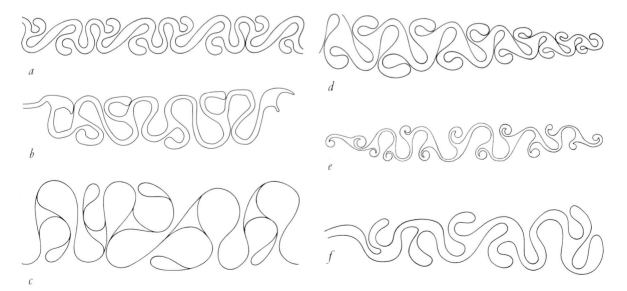

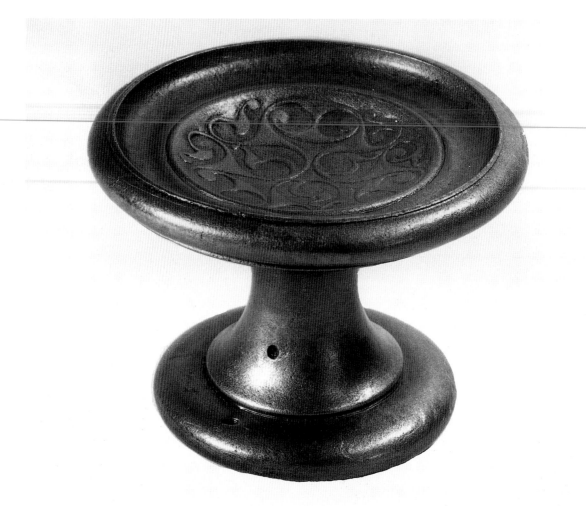

25 *Bronze 'horn-cap' from Brentford. Height 62 mm.*

26 Opposite *Terminal of the Grotesque Torque from Snettisham (see fig. 50).*

Stage III accounts for Jacobsthal's third Continental style, which he sub-divided into two contemporary developments, a 'Plastic Style' and 'Sword Style'. The 'Plastic Style', three dimensional high-relief ornament, in contrast to the linear or low-relief work of the Early, Waldalgesheim and Sword Styles, is still virtually unknown in Britain though it strongly influenced one major work, the 'Grotesque Torque' from Snettisham [26].

Likewise the influence of the Continental Sword Styles is seen in subsequent British developments, though close links are few. One major piece, the Ratcliffe shield-boss, was found in three pieces in the bed of the River Trent. Classified as horse-armour, it resided in the reserves of a provincial museum for many years before being acclaimed as a masterpiece of Early Celtic art in 1994 - a century after its discovery! The Waldalgesheim Style friezes bordering the spine have already been noted in Stage II (see fig. 24b), but the ornament on the central boss is an elaborate Sword Style creation, a complex of swirling tendrils emanating from a couple of fantastic beasts (see fig. 8). Of the four Waldalgesheim

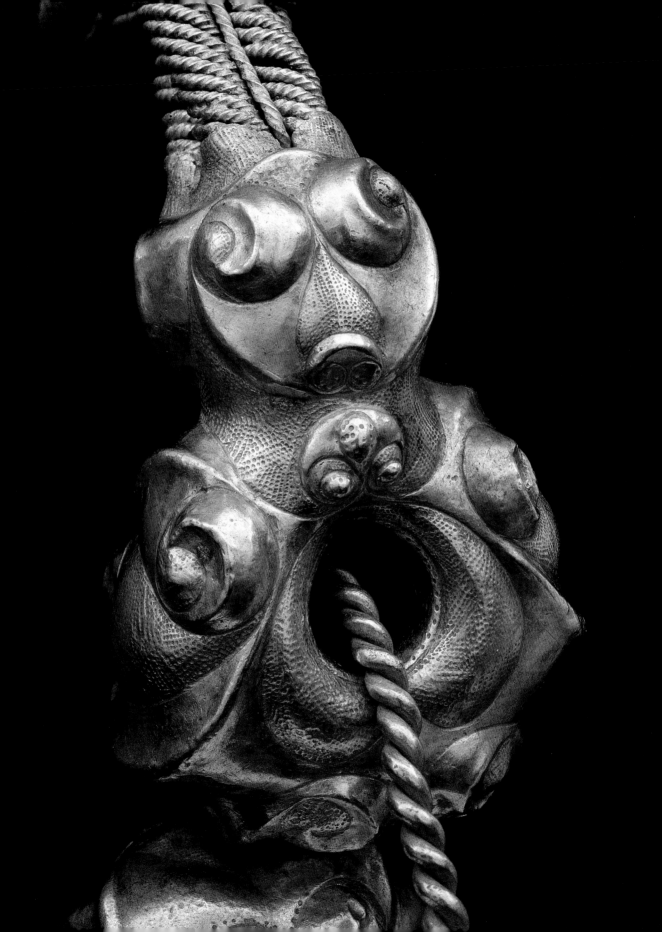

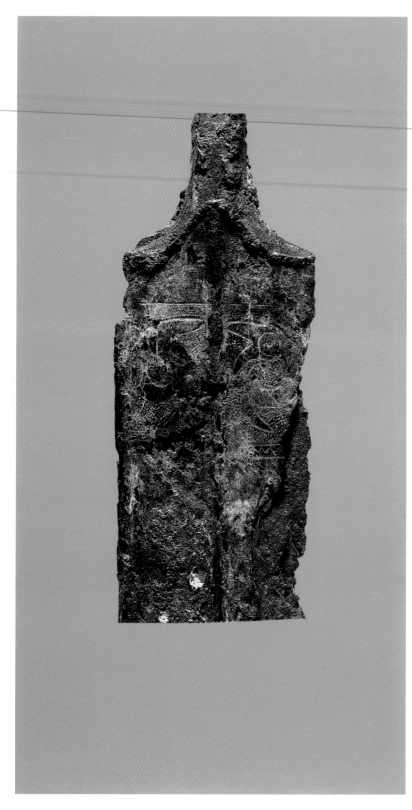

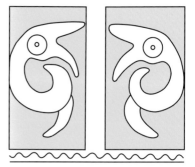

27 Upper part of an iron scabbard with dragon-pair ornament, from Hammersmith. Width of scabbard 51 mm.

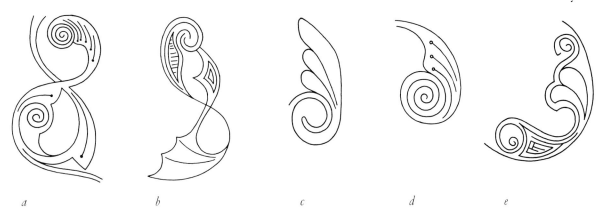

*a*          *b*          *c*          *d*          *e*

Style friezes, two terminate in very similar fantastic beasts. Two other British pieces with close Continental links had to wait even more than a hundred years before their significance was recognised. They are swords in scabbards, found in the River Thames in the middle of the nineteenth century, but their dragon-pair ornament was obscured until recent conservation work [27]. Dragon-pairs are confronted beasts engraved or chased towards the top of the scabbard. The significance of the design is unknown, of course, but it is difficult to believe that it was intended merely as decoration. In the third century BC, dragon-pairs appear on scabbards across Celtic Europe as far east as Romania and there are some quite remarkable similarities between examples from West and East. Despite their Oriental appearance the earliest dragon-pairs seem to occur in Western Europe, where they may well have originated in the lyre or confronted S-motif: some dragons are little more than an 'S' with an eye and an ear.

The Ratcliffe shield-boss and the Thames dragon-pairs show that there was a close link with Continental developments around 300 BC, but thereafter British art pursued an independent course. Stage IV belongs to the third century BC and includes masterpieces such as the shield and scabbard from the River Witham, and the two shield-bosses from the River Thames at Wandsworth. An important motif is the half-palmette, found already on works of the Continental 'Early Style', which features prominently on both pieces from the River Witham [28d, e]. The Witham scabbard was made of wood or leather that has now perished, but the magnificent bronze panel that decorated its mouth is still corroded onto the blade [29]. Beautifully preserved in bright shining

28 *Stage IV motifs. Comparable versions of a tendril crossing itself like a figure-of-eight: a) on the Witham shield; b) on the Wandsworth round-boss. The half-palmette: the derivation of c (an example from the cheek-piece of a helmet, probably from Italy) can be seen by reference to fig. 20a; d (on the Witham shield, cf. fig. 3) and e (on the Witham scabbard, cf. fig. 29) are more devolved versions.*

29 *Bronze ornament on a scabbard from the River Witham. Width 48 mm.*

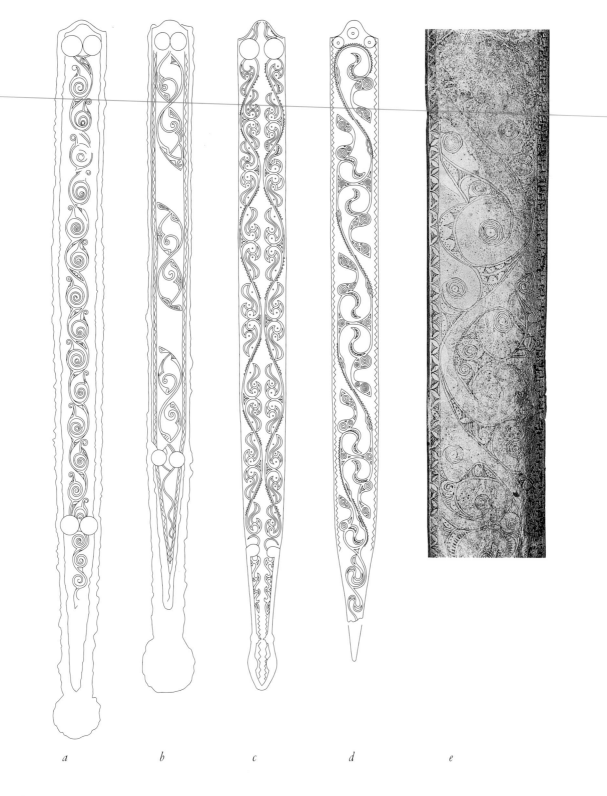

*a*　　　　*b*　　　　*c*　　　　*d*　　　　*e*

bronze, it is shaped in repoussé with an outline that crosses the sword diagonally like some of the Hungarian Sword Style designs. The overall shape of this panel may itself be a distorted half-palmette, and that motif certainly inspired some of the engraving that adorns it. Another distinctive feature is the tendril that crosses itself, a motif that occurs on both the Witham shield and the Wandsworth round-boss [28a, b]. It can be paralleled in Hungarian Sword Style ornament, and features prominently in the central design on the Ratcliffe shield-boss (see fig. 8).

The 'Witham-Wandsworth Style' is only one of the elments of Stage IV. The related Yorkshire and Irish 'Scabbard Styles' are based on S-motifs and wave-tendrils, some greatly elaborated and all enhanced with varied filler-motifs including tightly coiled spirals, triangular and lobe shapes, hatching and stippling [30]. Most of the designs are essentially symmetrical and repetitive, but one of the Bann scabbards has a variety of tendrils occupying every available space. The overall wave is

30 Opposite page *Yorkshire and Irish Scabbard Style art: a and b) Wetwang (East Yorks); c and d) Lisnacrogher (Co. Antrim); e) a length of the Bann scabbard (width 34 mm).*

31 *The 'bean-tin' from Wetwang (East Yorks). Diameter 87 mm.*

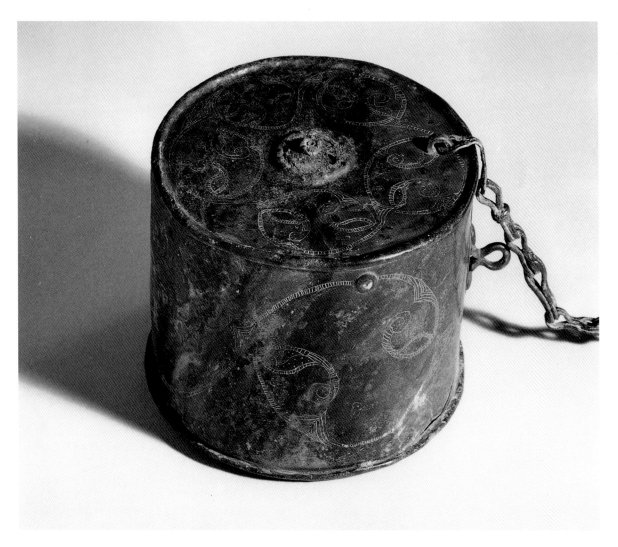

32 *Decoration at the mouth of the iron scabbard from Fovant (Wilts). Width 45 mm. Photograph of a replica.*

33 *Opposite page Bronze mirror, decorated on the back, from Aston (Herts). The mirror-plate was found by a farmer in 1979; the handle was discovered in a subsequent archaeological excavation. Width 194 mm.*

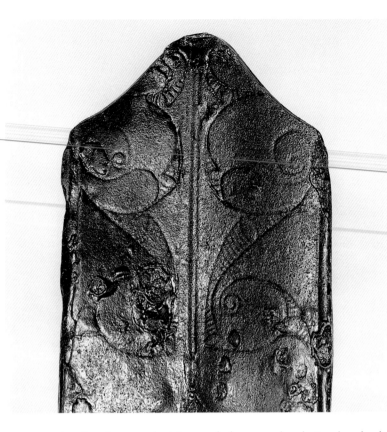

apparent despite the complexities, and there are bordering bands that recall the geometric borders of Late Hallstatt sheaths. The decorated scabbards have La Tène I chape-ends, derived from the Continent before the middle of the third century BC. But unlike Continental scabbards, those found in Yorkshire have central suspension loops, and that may have been the Irish practice too, which would suggest that the two Scabbard Styles diverged from an insular rather than a Continental tradition. There is one remarkable artefact decorated in the Scabbard Style that is not a scabbard. Made of sheet bronze and ornamented on every available surface, it looks like a cylindrical box, but it is completely sealed and has no lid [31]. It was found in the grave of a woman at Wetwang Slack (East Yorks) and the excavators called it the 'bean-tin' because it would take a tin-opener to get into it: its owner never needed to open it, perhaps because there was nothing inside.

There are hints of other regional styles in Stage IV, such as the iron scabbard from Fovant (Wilts) with a confronted motif surely derived from a dragon-pair [32]. But the graceful Fovant design is far removed from the mainly limited repertoire of Continental dragons, and its sprials and filler-motifs recall the decoration on the Bann scabbard. In eastern England another scabbard-plate, from Sutton (Notts), and a crown from Deal (see fig. 100) are decorated in related designs in which motifs are dissected and rearranged.

To Stage V belongs the art style studied especially by Sir Cyril Fox. He did not call it Stage V; indeed, he gave it no overall title, although one

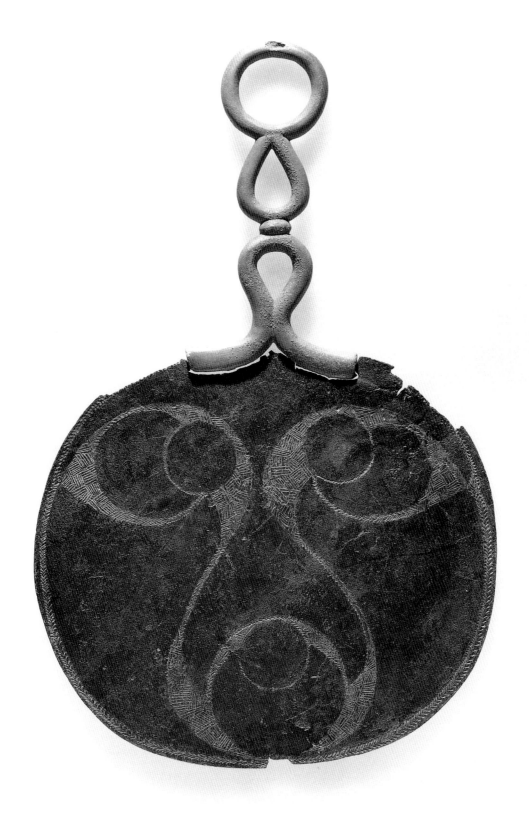

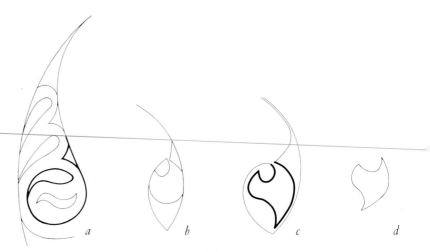

a b c d

34 *Diagrams showing how a lobe and cusp design (b and c), derived from a half-palmette (a), could give rise to a trumpet void (d): a) Saulces-Champenoises (Ardennes, France); b) Sutton (Notts); c) Wetwang (East Yorks).*

35 *Openwork sheet bronze cover for part of a shield-boss, from a grave at Deal (Kent). Length 99 mm.*

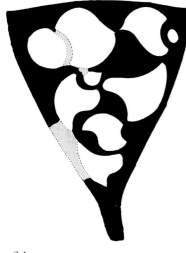

aspect of it he called the 'mirror-style'. His interest was aroused by the discovery in 1943 of a huge collection of metalwork at Llyn Cerrig Bach (Anglesey), acquired when he was the Director of the National Museum of Wales. The collection included two magnificent decorated bronzes, a plaque and a shield-boss, whose art-work was clearly related. In a series of publications Fox analysed the designs and traced the principal motifs in other works across Britain. He was keen to identify regional art styles (schools) and, by tracing the evolution and devolution of designs, he attempted to organise the material in a tight chronological order to which he applied tentative absolute dates.

Stage V includes tendril designs in elongated fields, as well as fragments of tendrils in minor panels and more ambitious designs in circular or rectangular frames. Shapes are more curvilinear than in Stage IV, fillings are confined to hatching (compare fig. 62 with fig. 30), used within the design or as background, and often the hatching is interrupted by a circle. Tendrils terminate not in a spiral, but in a distinctive 'trumpet' shape which, with an adjoining circle, gives the impression of a bird-head with huge eye and beak - sometimes an open beak [33]. The voids associated with these designs can be as distinctive as the pattern itself, and Fox drew attention to one particular shape, a 'trumpet' void constructed from three lines, one compound curve (concave/convex) and two simple curves (one concave and the other convex). This shape, seen in many Stage V designs, occurs already in the Yorkshire Scabbard Style (on the Kirkburn scabbard) and could have been derived from lobe and cusp designs which in turn evolve from half-palmettes [34]. In origin it was a negative shape, but it came to occupy a positive role as well. A shield-boss decorated with a random arrangement of trumpet voids was found in a grave at Mill Hill, Deal (Kent) and shows that the motif developed a life of its own as early as *c.* 200 BC [35].

Engraving and chasing were not the only means of producing Stage V patterns. Repoussé was popular, and the plaque from Llyn Cerrig Bach is a good example, with a design in a small circular panel and the repoussé executed in two planes [36]. The motif is basically a triskele or triquetra - a three-limbed device used throughout the history of Celtic art and perhaps best known on the Isle of Man coat of arms. On the plaque the

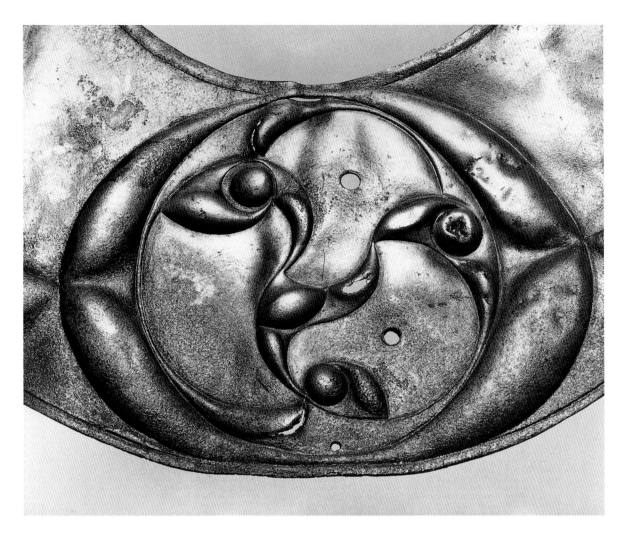

triskele is built from repoussé lobes; each limb ends in a 'trumpet' and a boss, and the whole is framed by lobes. On other pieces Stage V ornament is achieved by lost-wax casting, which can produce relief lobes and hatched backgrounds. Sometimes a single piece has ornament in different techniques, presumably made in the same workshop: the Bugthorpe (East Yorks) scabbard has engraved ornament on the front-plate and a decorated cast chape-end (see fig. 11), whereas a Little Wittenham (Oxon) scabbard combines lost-wax casting with repoussé.

With Stage V, in the second and first centuries BC, the comparatively isolated development of British art comes to an end in southern England. In the second half of the first century BC the neighbouring Gauls were under Roman control, and increasingly Britain was drawn into the same sphere. By Augustan times decorated Roman objects were in use and for the first time in the Iron Age there are undoubted imports from the Continent. In the north and in Scotland a distinctive art style continued to flourish, but workshops in the south of England copied Roman products, and British traditions were influenced by Roman taste.

*36 Repoussé decoration on a bronze plaque from Llyn Cerrig Bach. Note the three prominent 'trumpet voids' (as fig. 34d) defined by the repoussé shapes. Height 80 mm.*

# Chapter Three | Dress and jewellery

*T**HE GAULS** are tall in stature and their flesh is very moist and white, while their hair is not only naturally blond, but they also use artificial means to increase this natural quality of colour. For they continually wash their hair with lime-wash and draw it back from the forehead to the crown and to the nape of the neck ... the hair is so thickened by this treatment that it differs in no way from a horse's mane. Some shave off the beard, while others cultivate a short beard; the nobles shave the cheeks but let the moustache grow freely so that it covers the mouth.* (Diodorus Siculus)

The description by Diodorus Siculus contrasts with the modern image of the short dark Celt and illustrates the dangers of generalisations that ignore chronology and geography. Caesar confirms that the Britons too 'wear their hair long, and shave the whole of their bodies except the head and upper lip'. Very few British skeletons have been studied, and most of them are from Yorkshire, but they suggest that men were on average 1.69 m (5 ft 6½ in) tall and women 1.57 m (5 ft 2 in), while life expectancy was about thirty years, with only 8 per cent of the population over the age of forty-five. Representations of Britons include the bronze head on the handle of the North Grimston (North Yorks) sword, clean-shaven and with long hair down to the neck [37]. The three bronze heads from a burial at Welwyn (Herts) have their hair drawn back and sport impressive moustaches in accord with Caesar's description [38]. Bronze razors are known in Hallstatt times, but there are no La Tène razors in Britain until the end of the first century BC, when large triangular 'razor-knives' were

*37 Part of the bronze handle of a sword from North Grimston (North Yorks). Height of head, 28 mm.*

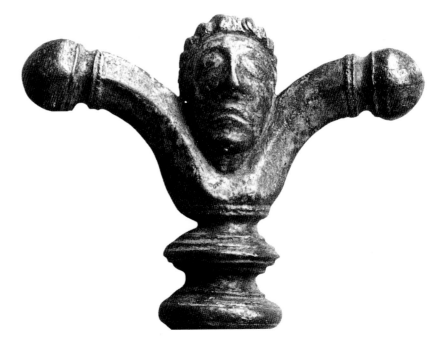

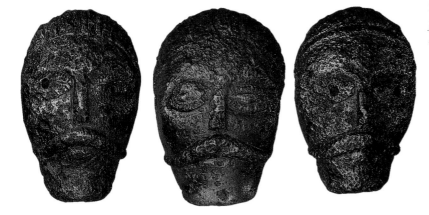

used. The shears with which they must have cut their hair are rarely found before the end of the first century BC, when they occur in graves at Hertford Heath (Herts) and Alkham (Kent).

'All the Britons dye their bodies with *vitrum*, which produces a blue colour, and this gives them a more terrifying appearance in battle.' Caesar's observation is expanded by Herodian, describing the natives of north Britain in the third century AD: 'they mark their bodies with various figures of all kinds of animals and wear no clothes for fear of concealing these figures'. Caesar's word 'vitrum' is usually translated as woad, an important source of blue dye in more recent times, but that is by no means certain. It has been argued that two ancient bodies from Lindow Moss (see p. 86) were painted with a copper-based pigment that might have been Caesar's 'vitrum'. But even if the Lindow bodies were painted, no patterns can be distinguished now. What might have been a common British art-form has disappeared without trace.

According to Diodorus Siculus, the Gauls 'wear a striking kind of clothing - tunics dyed and stained in various colours, and trousers, which they call by the name of bracae; and they wear striped cloaks, fastened with buckles, thick in winter and light in summer, picked out with a variegated small check pattern'. Very occasionally fabric has been preserved, either in waterlogged conditions or where the structure of small pieces of cloth has been replaced by corrosion products from adjoining metal artefacts. Replaced fabric on an iron brooch from Burton Fleming (East Yorks) showed a complex construction of stripes and diamond twill with some details added by needle, making it one of the earliest attempts at embroidery known from England.

Of the dress described by Diodorus Siculus the most that the archaeologist can expect to find is the buckle, or brooch, which fastened the cloak. Although there are Hallstatt brooches in Britain, types that are commonly found in Italy, not one comes from an undoubtedly ancient context and they may be comparatively recent imports. Instead, bronze or iron pins were used. But from about 400 BC La Tène brooches are fairly frequent: some were perhaps imported, though the vast majority must have been manufactured locally. Such brooches were usually bronze, and the prototypes were made in one piece. The decorative body

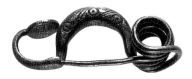

would be cast; then a projection from the head would be hammered and drawn into a long wire to form the spring and pin. The spring was coiled first to the right of the bow and then to the left, always in the same way so that the pin was engaged in a catch-plate on the left side of the brooch. From the catch-plate extends a foot which turns back to the bow; both foot and bow are sometimes decorated in the original casting and occasionally, especially on the foot, provision is made for an applied knob of coral or 'enamel' inlay. Iron brooches were made to the same pattern, but were entirely forged and not cast. This La Tène I type of brooch was popular for a couple of centuries, and then the design was improved by lengthening the free end of the foot, which was liable to get bent and broken, and clasping it to the bow with a separate collar, a development distinguishing the La Tène II brooch. It was then a short step, although it took about a century to achieve it, to cast or forge the bow and the end of the foot together in one piece, the distinctive feature of the La Tène III brooch. This classic typological sequence is used to distinguish the three stages of La Tène chronology [39], but it does not accommodate all La Tène brooches, and Britain in particular has several peculiarities.

The manufacturers of British La Tène brooches occasionally used springs in the Continental fashion, but they also experimented with various hinge mechanisms. In one of the more popular forms the bow terminated in a single ring which superficially resembles the coil of a spring; the pin was manufactured separately with two linked coils to fit on either side of that ring and the junction was secured by a rivet. Other British brooches had a pin simply pivoted between two projecting lugs. But the hinge was not the only British peculiarity, for at a comparatively early stage the foot was cast in one with the bow. This development, which distinguishes the La Tène III brooch on the Continent, is seen in the much

39 *A typological sequence of British La Tène bronze brooches: I, Wood Eaton (Oxon); II, Wetwang (East Yorks); III Unprovenanced. Lengths 47, 69 and 67 mm.*

40 *Bronze and coral brooch from the Queen's Barrow, Arras (East Yorks). Length 66 mm.*

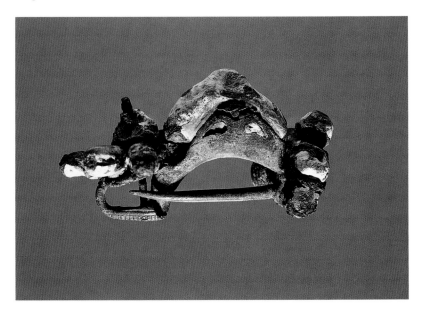

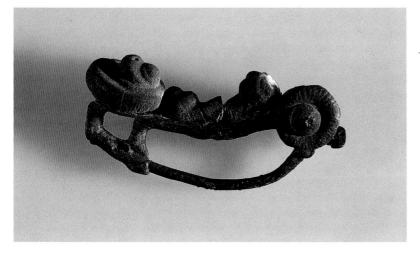

41 *Bronze brooch with red-coloured sandstone ornament, from Danes Graves (East Yorks). Length 65 mm.*

earlier Queen's Barrow at Arras (East Yorks), where the brooch is otherwise of La Tène I shape and has elaborate ornament suggesting influence from the La Tène I 'Münsingen' brooch on the Continent [40]. Many British La Tène II bronze brooches have the foot and bow cast in one piece, although iron brooches were still made with a foot which had to be secured to the bow by a collar.

The distinctive 'involuted' brooch developed in Britain in La Tène II and may have lasted into the early years of the first century BC. The bows on some British brooches of La Tène I form were much flatter than those fashionable on the Continent, and they seem to have given rise to the involuted brooch. When securing the pin in its catch-plate it would be natural to press down on the centre of the bow, and a long flat bow could easily become down-curved, or involuted [41]. Many brooches were deliberately manufactured in this way, and an interesting sequence of graves at Wetwang Slack (East Yorks) has shown how the long involuted brooch was gradually superseded by a shorter and more curved variety.

In the first century BC, and especially after Caesar's expeditions, British brooches again came under the influence of the Continental tradition. New forms may have been imported, perhaps including some of the silver brooches found in cemeteries in south-eastern England: they resemble Italian silver brooches, and were used at a time when other Italian imports were certainly reaching Britain. But other La Tène III brooches in Britain are sufficiently distinctive to show that there must have been a flourishing native industry. Brooches were now occasionally worn in pairs, sometimes linked by a chain, in a way known on the Continent since the fifth century BC. By the first century AD brooches of many types were in common use all over southern England: few of them have other than the simplest decoration, but occasionally an elaborate Celtic design is found. The most ornate is the surprisingly large gilt-bronze brooch from Aesica (the Latin name for Great Chesters, Northumberland) found in a small hoard of jewellery in 1894 [42]. Records of the discovery are unsatisfactory, but the hoard seems to have been concealed at the end of the third century AD, although the brooch

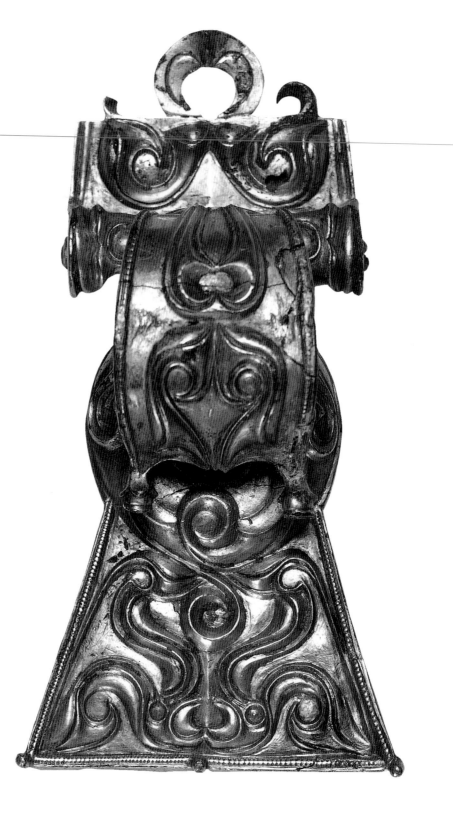

was probably made two hundred years earlier. 'Of its kind probably the most fantastically beautiful creation that has come to us from antiquity', enthused Sir Arthur Evans, but to J.M. de Navarro it was 'rather flamboyant, not to say vulgar'.

Pins are a simpler form of dress-fastening, used in Britain before the introduction of the brooch and not completely ousted in La Tène times, though they were quite rare. There were only four pins from the 446 burials at Wetwang Slack, two of them in one grave, and no cemetery has produced more. The finest pins are quite long and have ornamental heads, often ring-heads, and a 'swan's neck' bend in the stem [43]. Two

42 Opposite *The gilt-bronze Aesica brooch. Length 103 mm.*

43 *A bronze pin with coral ornament, from Danes Graves. Length 126 mm.*

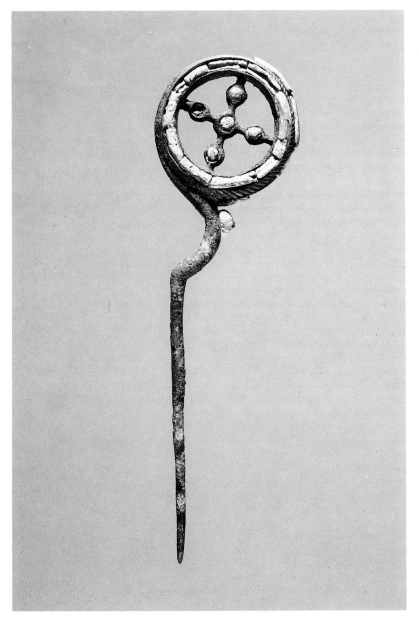

ornate pins from Yorkshire graves were found immediately adjoining the skulls, suggesting that they may have been hair-pins, but because of the way in which the skeletons had been bundled up, a dress fastening from the upper part of the body could easily have fallen by the skull.

Bracelets were occasionally worn, but they were far less common than brooches: whereas up to a third of the Yorkshire burials were accompanied by a brooch, no more than 5 per cent had a bracelet [44]. The finest bracelets were made of bronze and some had decorative settings for inlay. They fitted fairly closely round the wrist so various devices had to be used to allow them to be pushed over the hand: some had a simple opening in one side, others had a projection at one end of the break to fit in a hole at the other (a mortice-and-tenon fitting) and a third type had overlapping terminals. A few shale or jet bracelets have been found, and some made of iron belonged to the later stages of the Wetwang Slack cemetery. The bracelets in these Yorkshire cemeteries were always worn by women, but according to classical writers bracelets were worn by both men and women in Gaul. The cremation at Snailwell (Cambs) seems to have been that of a male; the grave-goods included a shield-boss and a razor-knife, but one of the finest objects found there was a spirally twisted bracelet with 'snake-head' terminals [45]. This is the only bracelet of its type from England, though there are others from Scotland. A related type is the 'massive armlet', found only in Scotland and Ireland, cast by the lost-wax process and sometimes with enamel or glass ornament in the terminals [46]. The decoration of the metalwork is consistent with other pieces from northern England and Scotland dating from the end of the first century and the second century AD. They have never been found on a skeleton and

*44 Bracelets from Cowlam (centre front) and Burton Fleming; (East Yorks): the one on the left is made of jet (diameter 84 mm) and the others are bronze (diameters c.60 mm).*

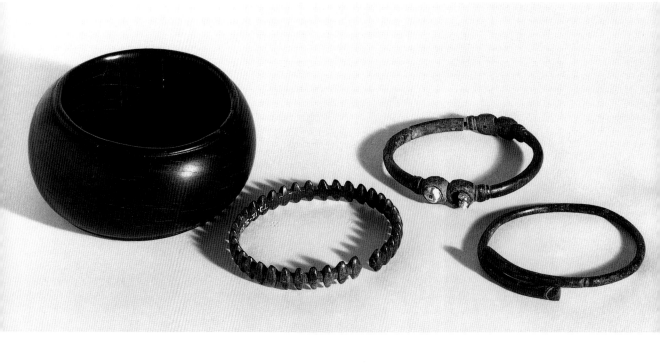

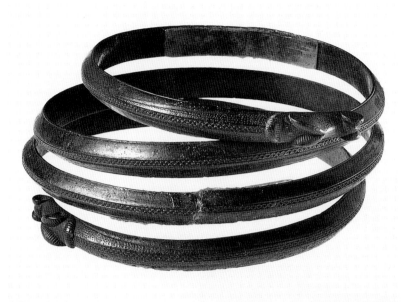

indeed these ungainly objects could perhaps have been intended for gods rather than people. Conceivably they could have been worn round the ankle. Anklets were certainly worn on the Continent and one is supposed to have been found on one of the Arras skeletons.

In the Wetwang Slack cemetery more than 500 glass beads were found, most of them in 10 different necklaces: 80 per cent of the beads were plain and only 6 per cent contained colours other than blue. Three other Yorkshire skeletons had bead necklaces, including one from Cowlam that has one large bead decorated with inset white rings and sixty-nine with white scrolls. White ornament on a blue base was popular and circles were created either by insetting annulets in channelled rings or by inserting a white disc in a hollow and superimposing a central blue dot ('stratified eye bead'). All the types of beads found so far in Yorkshire are represented in the necklace from the Queen's Barrow at Arras, including translucent beads with a greenish tinge decorated with white or yellow scrolls [47]. Of the 100 beads said to have made up the necklace when found, 67 still survive.

The majority of the Yorkshire burials are without grave-goods and the rest are but poorly equipped. The Queen's Barrow group, however, is comparatively rich. Found in 1816 in a shallow grave under a small barrow, the skeleton had been adorned with the necklace of glass beads, an amber ring, bronze and coral brooch (see fig. 40), two bronze bracelets, a bronze and coral pendant or belt-fitting and the only gold finger-ring from Iron Age Britain, now unfortunately lost. Finger-rings of any metal are rare; curiously, toe-rings seem to have been more common.

One object often associated with the Celts is the torque: mentioned

45 *Bronze bracelet from Snailwell (Cambs). Diameter 105 mm.*

46 *Bronze armlets with enamel ornament, from Castle Newe (Aberdeenshire) and (right) Drummond Castle (Perthshire). Diameters 141 and 147 mm.*

several times by classical writers, it is also shown on representations, and found in graves and hoards. The torque is a collar, or neck-ring, and its name comes from one of the more common varieties, the hoop of which is a twisted strand of metal: a Roman, T. Manlius, took a collar from a Celtic warrior and earned himself the cognomen of Torquatus. At the Battle of Telemon 'all the warriors in the front ranks were adorned in gold necklaces and bracelets' (Polybius), and that was not an isolated occurrence. But in Celtic graves torques are usually associated with women rather than warriors, and are made of bronze, rarely of iron, but hardly ever of gold. On the Continent they are best known from graves in Champagne, where they were extremely popular until La Tène II, but then they became rare and they are never found with La Tène III burials.

In Britain torques are absent from graves. The Yorkshire inhumations have bead necklaces instead, and the La Tène III cremations in south-eastern England resemble contemporary cremations in northern France and the Rhineland and have no torques. But their absence from graves does not mean that they were not worn by some of the Britons, for there is a rich collection of material - often gold - from other sources. Gold torques must have been valuable always, and thus vulnerable: when

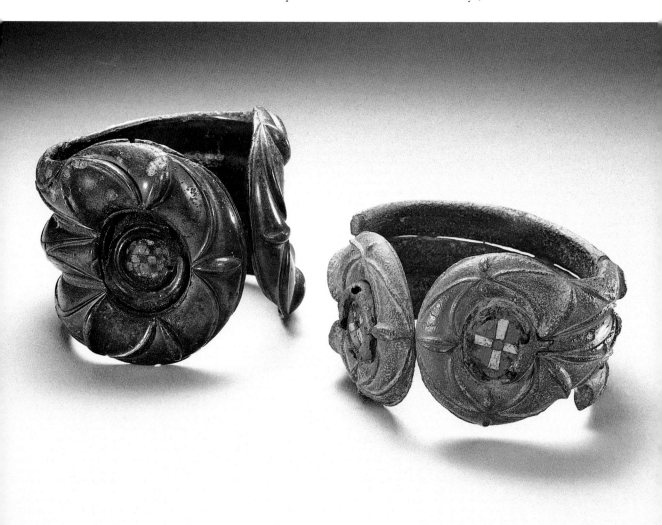

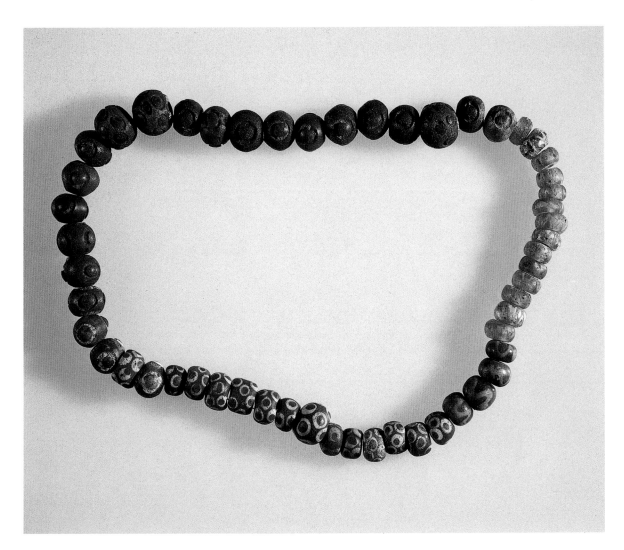

they were broken, damaged or unfashionable they would have been melted down, and it is hardly surprising that they are not found in graves. They found their way into the metalsmith's crucible in recent as well as ancient times: the surviving fragments from Clevedon (Avon) are the remains of a find made before 1897 and 'mostly melted by Parson & Son, Bristol' [48]. A most unusual burial was said to have been found at Mildenhall (Suffolk) in 1812 - 'a human skeleton of large dimensions, stretched at its full length between the skeletons of two horses ... on one side of the warrior lay a long iron sword, on the other his celt: he had a torque of gold' - but the torque was immediately melted down by a silversmith at Bury St Edmunds.

The gold torques that do survive, however, are very impressive. One found at Broighter (Co. Derry) in 1896 is a magnificent piece of work which has a somewhat chequered history [49]. Found by a ploughman with a curious assemblage of other gold objects, two torques of different types, a model boat, a bowl and two fine chain necklaces, it was

47 *Necklace of glass beads from the Queen's Barrow, Arras (East Yorks).*

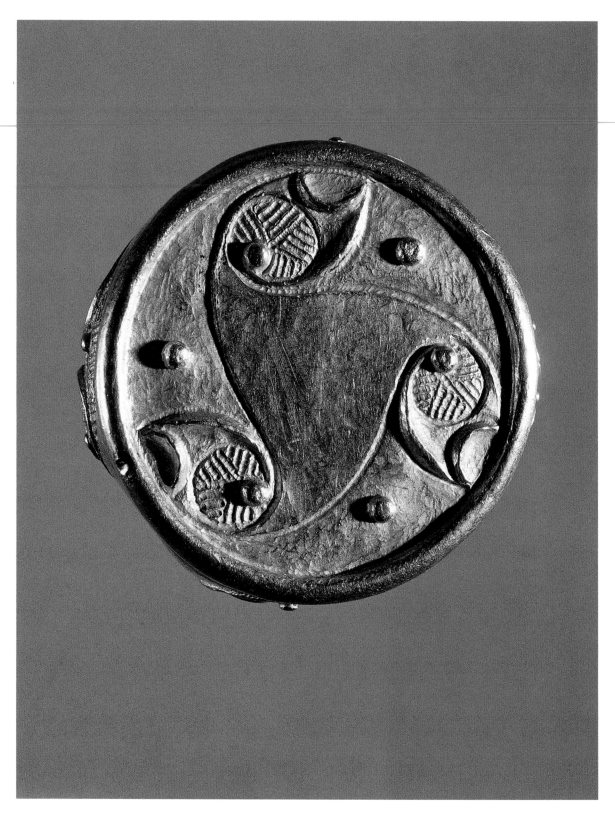

bought by the British Museum but then claimed as Treasure Trove by the Royal Irish Academy. A famous trial at the Royal Courts of Justice in London in 1903 decided in favour of the Irish and the collection is now exhibited at Dublin. Subsequently one reputable archaeologist claimed that the hoard had been collected and buried in the nineteenth century, and another declared that it had been found in an old umbrella in a ditch! But the authenticity of the association is now generally accepted, and there is no doubt at all that the torque is a genuine La Tène antiquity. It is made of two hollow tubes whose terminals are linked by a swivel-joint that can be opened by turning one half through 90 degrees, and there would have been a decorative 'muff' to secure the two ends at the back. The rich chased decoration (not repoussé) seems to have been executed before the tubes were shaped. The high-relief 'snail-shells' have been separately applied, and the background to the design has been covered by fine arcs for which the compass-points can still be distinguished.

Three rather similar but less ornate tubular torques, one large and two small, were found with the remains of a fourth torque in a field at Snettisham (Norfolk) in 1948. Each had a tubular body, made in two halves like the Broighter torque, with buffer terminals and a band to cover the joint at the back. That field at Snettisham produced five hoards in the course of deep-ploughing in the autumns of 1948 and 1950: four of them were within 25 m of one another and the fifth was about 55 m away. Between 1964 and 1973 four isolated torques were found in the course of agricultural work, and after that it seemed very likely that the site had been completely wrecked by ploughing. But in 1989 Charles Hodder, of Kings Lynn, started to survey the field with his metal detector, and in his second season he struck gold. He discovered a hoard of mainly broken gold and silver artefacts, with a total weight of 9.2 kg. Clearly the

48 Opposite *The terminal of the Clevedon torque, with a triskele motif. Diameter 34 mm.*

49 *Gold torque from Broighter. Diameter 195 mm.*

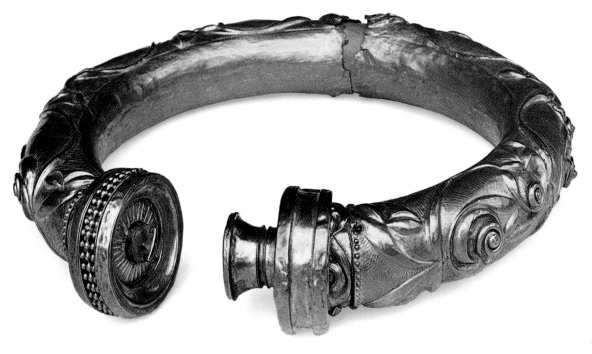

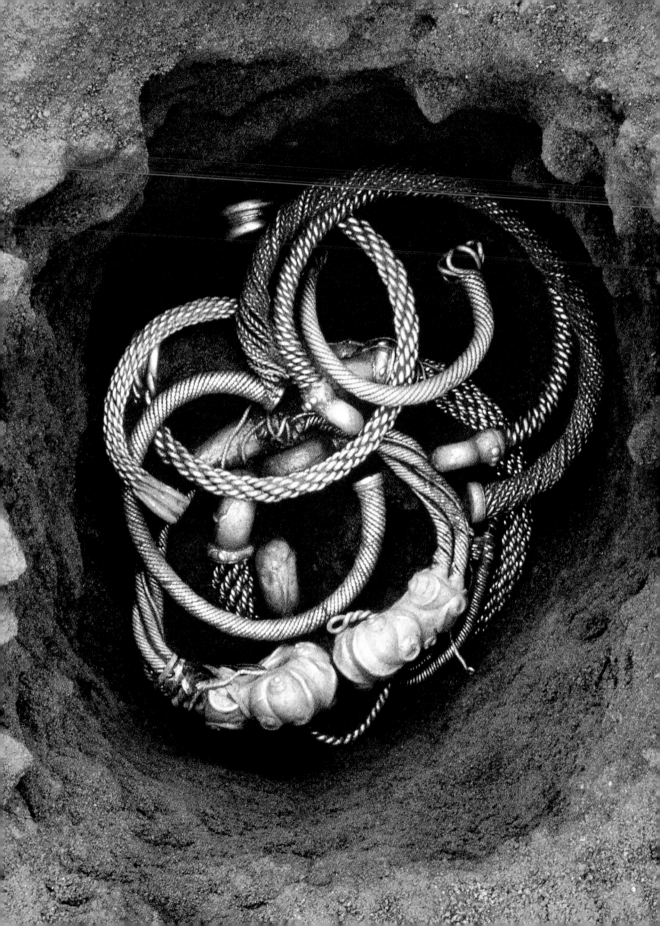

site had not been completely wrecked by ploughing. With the enthusiastic support of the landowner, Sir Stephen Lycett-Green, and the active participation of Charles Hodder, the British Museum launched an immediate excavation and found five more hoards [50]. Subsequently Hodder discovered a hoard of silver lumps, and a clandestine metal detectorist made off with a huge hoard of coins.

The 'Gold Field' at Snettisham has produced at least 12 and perhaps 14 hoards, including 75 more or less complete torques and fragments of 100 more. The entire treasure, some 20 kg of silver and 15 kg of gold, is surely more than the savings of an individual and must represent the wealth of a community. Perhaps it was a tribal treasury. Extensive excavations in the immediate vicinity of the hoards failed to locate any evidence of contemporary activity, but they did identify a huge 8-hectare enclosure defined by a ditch. It was not possible to date the construction of the enclosure, but the ditch had been abandoned and allowed to silt about AD 100, more than a century and a half after the torques had been deposited. It is tempting to relate the enclosure to the torques that were found near its centre; the ditch was not an impressive defensive work but it might have defined an area that had had more

50 Opposite page *Hoard of gold torques found at Snettisham in 1990. They are photographed in the pit, as found, before they were moved.*

51 *The Great Torque from Snettisham. Diameter 199 mm.*

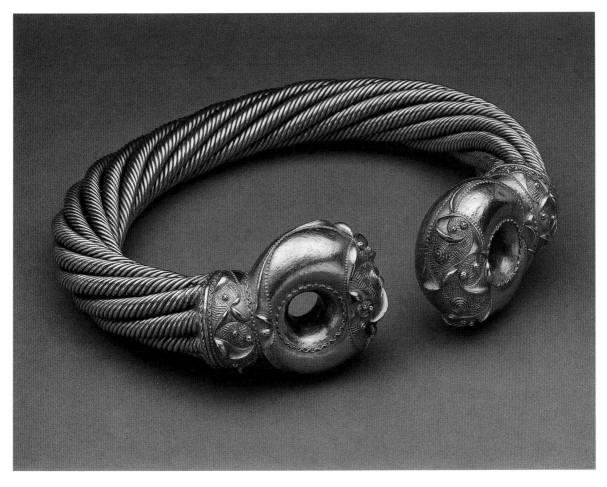

formidible defenders, such as ghosts or gods. Whatever its function, the Snettisham site lost its significance in the first century AD and the Britons never recovered their treasure.

The multi-strand torque from Hoard E at Snettisham, the Great Torque [51], is one of Britain's finest antiquities. Its hoop is made of eight strands twisted together, and each strand in turn comprises eight lengths of swaged wire. The ends of the wires have been secured in hollow terminals made by the lost-wax process. The decoration on the terminals, which would have been modelled in the wax, is formed by low-relief lobes, some of which define trumpet voids with matted hatching. Details, including the small knobs with triple dots, show a close relationship with the terminal of a similar torque from nearby Sedgeford and more surprisingly with a comparable terminal from Cairnmuir in Scotland. A small Gaulish coin trapped within the Snettisham torque (but not necessarily deliberately concealed by the manufacturer, as originally reported) is contemporary with other coins from the site and supports that notion that all the torques were buried about the same time.

A hoard of five torques was found at Ipswich (Suffolk) in 1968, when a machine was moving earth on a new housing estate: a sixth torque found two years later in a nearby garden may have been displaced from the original hoard [52]. They were made of a gold alloy (on average 80

*52 The Ipswich torques. Diameters 181 to 197 mm.*

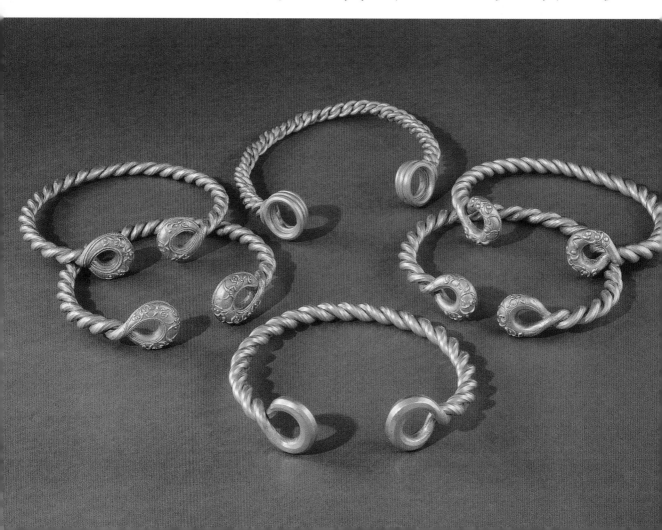

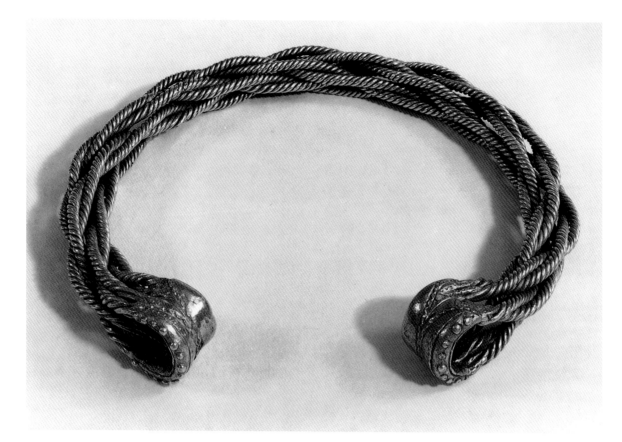

per cent gold) and five of them are quite similar, with twisted hoops and loop terminals, one undecorated and four with relief designs like those on the Great Torque. But the sixth torque is different, with ring terminals and a more complex twist, and it may be no coincidence that it was found apart from the others. Experiments showed how the torques with loop terminals would have been constructed: from a cast ingot a long faceted wire was formed, bent in half, and the two strands twisted together; the terminals were then cast-on using the lost-wax process. Two of the decorated torques were left 'as cast' from the mould, but the other two were worked over with a tracer which has obscured most of the tool-marks modelled in the wax. East Anglia is not the only source of gold torques, but the only other marked concentration is in Staffordshire, where they have been found on four sites within 20 miles of one another. Two of the torques in this group, from Glascote and Needwood Forest, have multi-strand hoops onto which broad loop terminals have been cast [53]. Like most surviving gold torques in England they seem to date from the first century BC. But torques were still used in the middle of the following century, according to the description of Queen Boudicca given by Dio Cassius: 'in stature she was very tall, in appearance most terrifying, in the glance of her eye most fierce, and her voice was harsh; a great mass of the tawniest hair fell to her hips; around her neck was a large golden necklace'.

*53 Gold torque from Needwood Forest. Diameter 179 mm.*

# Chapter Four | Hearth and home

*T**HEIR HOUSES** are large and circular, built of planks and wickerwork, the roof being a dome of heavy thatch.* (Strabo)

Strabo's description of a Gallic house might well be applied to Britain, but such structures leave little trace for the archaeologist. Remains of domestic architecture are restricted to plans of circular huts usually from 5 to 9 m in diameter, but some up to 15 m, in the form of a ring of post-holes or a rough stone foundation course, and the only refinements are the occasional porch and a trench to divert rain-water. Very occasionally finds add a touch of colour, as in the hillfort at Hod Hill (Dorset), where some huts had collections of sling-stones, presumably once in bags, stored ready for action by the doorway, and one hut thought to belong to a chieftain had a spearhead in a similar position. Perhaps the buildings were decorated inside with fabric wall-hangings, but these and any other fitments have long since perished and significant artefacts are limited to the latch-lifter that opened the door. Of furniture there was probably very little: in Gaul 'when dining they all sit not in chairs, but on the earth' and 'their custom is to sleep on the ground upon the skins of wild animals' (Diodorus Siculus). Animal skins must include those of the brown bear, because two cremations in southern England produced terminal phalanges - the claws that would have been left in a treated skin.

The Gauls dined next to 'hearths blazing with fire, with cauldrons and spits containing large pieces of meat' (Diodorus Siculus); here metal artefacts come more into the picture. Iron fire-dogs are known especially from graves in south-eastern England, a ritual deposition that gives no idea of their original distribution [54]. They were used in pairs like their recent counterparts, to contain the logs of the fire. But the Iron Age hearth was in the centre of the room, not against the wall, and the fire-dogs could be viewed from all sides so they had a head at each end. Their exceptionally long necks have never been satisfactorily explained: an elaborate example from Capel Garmon (Gwynedd) has loops at either end of the uprights which could have held cross-bars to support spits, but no other fire-dog has such attachments. A curious iron frame found in a La Tène III grave at Welwyn (Herts) looks

54 *Iron fire-dog from Welwyn. Height 970/985 mm.*

55 *Iron frame from Welwyn. Height 1.43 m.*

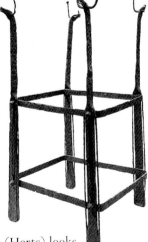

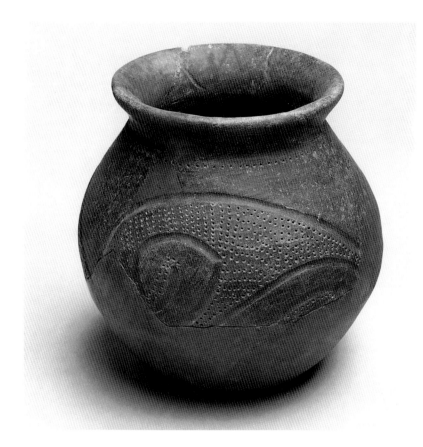

like a pair of fire-dogs linked together and has two tiers of cross-struts [55]. Perhaps it was used as a brazier, although it would have needed gridded walls and floor; certainly it should in some way be connected with a fire. Several bronze cauldrons are known, one associated with fire-dogs in a grave at Baldock (Herts), while a grave at Stanfordbury (Beds) included an iron tripod from which a cauldron had been suspended.

Throughout the British Iron Age jars and bowls were made of pottery. Many of them must have been made in the home, but some of the finer wares were produced professionally and traded. Decoration is usually unambitious but some of the professional products have incised scrolls and curvilinear patterns with shapes infilled with hatching or stippling [56]. After Caesar's expeditions to Britain trade with Gaul was increased and fine table-ware came onto the British market.

Italian wine was imported from the end of the second century BC, in tall pottery amphorae, found in sherds on settlements and sometimes complete in graves [57]. Diodorus Siculus reported that the Gauls were 'exceedingly fond of wine and sate themselves with the unmixed wine imported by merchants; their desire makes them drink it greedily and when they become drunk they fall into a stupor or into a maniacal disposition'. Doubtless the Britons were affected in the same way, but as time went on they adopted some of the refinements of the Romans. The new drink could be better appreciated in an Italian silver cup: several were

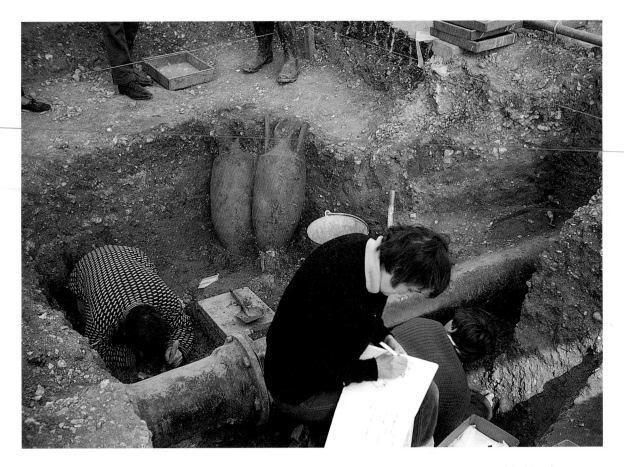

57 *The excavation of a rich La Tène III burial at Welwyn Garden City in 1965. A gas-pipe trench had destroyed part of the grave but most of the grave-goods were recovered and a complete plan was reconstructed. The grave measured 3.2 by 2.2 m and contained five amphorae, two of them still in position when this photograph was taken. For glass game-pieces from this burial see fig. 99.*

imported towards the end of the first century BC, and half a dozen survive. But British metalworkers did not attempt to copy them. The principal native drinking-vessel of the time was the tankard, made of wood banded with bronze, furnished with a cast bronze handle, and better suited to native beer. Merchants provided those who preferred wine with the means of serving it: not only a bronze jug but also a long-handled pan in which it could be warmed. The Roman drinking service would not have been complete without a bucket in which the wine was mixed, but it seems that this item was not traded to Britain. In a grave at Aylesford (Kent) an imported bronze jug and pan were accompanied by a Celtic bronze-bound wooden bucket whose final use had been as the depository for the cremated bones [58]. A pair of comparable vessels from a grave at Baldock (Herts) was associated with an Italian amphora, and it is tempting to see the type as the native equivalent of a wine-mixing bucket. The Aylesford grave was discovered in a gravel pit in 1886 and the finds were shown to Arthur Evans, who was visiting the site with his father in search of Stone Age implements. The bucket had not been excavated under the best of circumstances, but the rim, uppermost bronze band, internal bronze band, handle-mounts and handle held together in one piece, with fragments of wooden staves trapped between the bronze bands. The arrangement of the lower part of the bucket is not so certain, but on the strength of a tiny decorated fragment and on the analogy of other British and Continental examples it can be equipped with three feet. The bronze-bound iron handle pivots in holes in the back of two cast bronze handle-mounts, each in the form of a helmeted human head; they had been dismantled and reattached twice, suggesting some antiquity for the bucket before it was buried. The upper band has relief ornament produced in formers (see fig. 7), and the most interesting design is a pair of confronted animals based on horses, or perhaps stags, created by an artist not unduly worried by details of anatomy. These fantastic animals have antlers, curling lips, bifurcating devil-like tails, and human knees. At Marlborough (Wilts) a cremation was found in a far grander vessel, which had capacity of about eight times that of the Aylesford bucket. It was recorded and lifted by the Revd Charles Francis about 1807: a 'drawing was made on the spot while it was entire', but 'it would not bear the smallest jar or shake, and it fell to pieces'. According to the original drawing there were three decorated bands, but only fragments survive.

*58 The Aylesford bucket; for a detail of the animals on the upper band see fig. 7. Height (excluding the helmeted handle-mounts) 300 mm.*

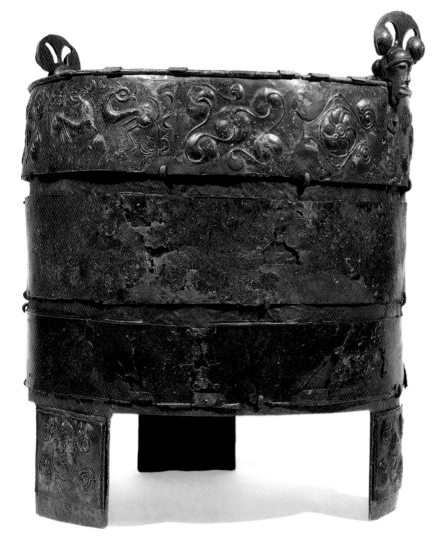

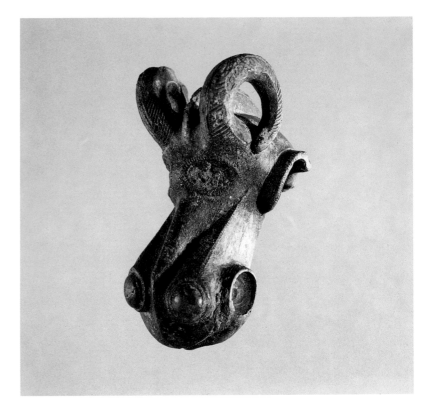

Fantastic animals have been seen on sword scabbards of the third century BC and there are faces in the designs of the Wandsworth mask shield and the Witham shield (which once carried a long-legged boar, see fig. 3), but fairly naturalistic renderings of animals, like humans, are rare before the first century BC. From Felmersham (Beds) comes a pair of handle-mounts in the form of cows' heads [59]. They were cast by the lost-wax process and are slightly different from one another: the difference is quite deliberate in that only one of the cows' heads has an outstretched tongue licking its muzzle. From the back of the casting a stout rivet projects to attach the mount to a wooden bucket, and on top of the head is a ring to take the end of the handle. There are several other bovine handle fittings, and Fox suggested that they might have belonged to milk pails: all the more reason for the helmeted heads from Aylesford, Baldock and Alkham (see figs 74 and 75) to have presided over a much more potent brew. There are few representations of animals other than cows and bulls, but a fine pair of rams' heads, also bucket escutcheons, was found in what seems to have been a disturbed grave at Harpenden (Herts) [60]. They are powerfully modelled, each with hollow oval eyes perhaps once inlaid with 'enamel', a long bony snout and large circular settings for 'enamel' at the nostrils, the sides of the mouth and perhaps at the back of the head as well.

59 *A cow licking its muzzle, a bronze escutcheon from a bucket, found at Felmersham. The span of the horns is 46 mm.*

60 *A ram's head, a bronze escutcheon from a bucket, found at Harpenden. Height 75 mm.*

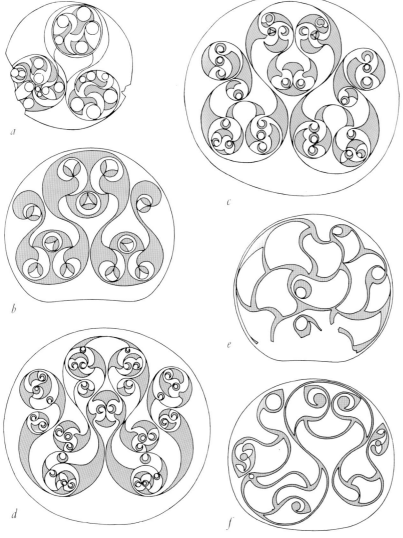

61 *Decoration on the backs of bronze mirrors: a) Mayer Collection; b) Colchester; c) Birdlip; d) Holcombe; e) Old Warden; f) Great Chesterford.*

Classical writers speak of the vanity of the Celts, and Strabo comments on the beauty of the women. Their houses may not have been equipped with much furniture, but they had the luxury of admiring themselves in mirrors. Iron mirrors were in use as early as the third century BC, then bronze mirrors became fashionable. Information is restricted because the surviving sample depends on burial practices. Mirrors are usually found in graves, and their absence from the south of England before the end of the first century BC is due in part to the rarity of burials there before Caesar's expeditions. The bronze mirror was a luxury item, offering scope for decoration not only in its cast handle but also on the flat field of the mirror-plate itself. The viewing surface was polished and plain, but its back was often covered with elaborate line-work; when not in use it may well have been hung on the wall, in which case the decorated side would normally have been seen with the handle at the top.

62 Opposite page *The Desborough mirror. Length 350 mm.*

Mirror decoration was studied and perceptively analysed by Sir Cyril Fox, who saw the development of the decoration in terms of a typological sequence evolved from the triskele within a circle as seen on the Llyn Cerrig Bach repoussé plaque (see fig. 36). The designs were sometimes enclosed in two or three adjoining circles; more often the circles merged into a scroll but a tripartite arrangement could be distinguished in all but the most devolved examples. Fox saw 'a familiar evolution of art forms' spanning less than a century: 'if Mayer [61a] may be regarded as archaic, Colchester with its severe and regular structure [61b] is classic; Birdlip [61c] may be held to correspond to the 'decorated' phase of medieval, the 'baroque' phase of renaissance art; Desborough [62] is clearly to be defined as 'flamboyant', less justly perhaps as 'rococo'.' But he treated his sequence too seriously when it came to assigning dates, suggesting limits of AD 5-20 for the Great Chesterford mirror [61f] and AD 1-15 for the one from Colchester [61b]. The few mirrors that can be dated seem to belong to the century after Caesar's expeditions, but it is difficult to justify any sequence of evolution.

Detailed study of the construction of the designs, by a team led by Richard Savage, has enabled the marks of various tools to be identified (see fig. 9). Only on the Mayer mirror was the standard of craftsmanship so high that it was impossible to tell whether the design had been chased or engraved. The Mayer design was constructed with compasses, but free-hand scratched 'guidelines' can be distinguished, and it is difficult to understand their function. Some of the work, as on the Holcombe mirror, was meticulous and time-consuming, but other examples, such as Old Warden [61e], have uneven outlines and rough hatching carried out quickly using a tool with a broken edge. From a technical point of view the mirrors seem to group geographically, with a series of related pieces along the Jurassic belt from Devon via Gloucestershire to Northamptonshire, and a second group to the south-east from Buckinghamshire and Bedfordshire across to Essex. Detailed study of the marks of tools is an approach which falls short of identifying the work of individual craftsmen, but it reveals a great deal about the construction and execution of designs.

The decorated mirror is one of the highlights of Celtic art, and a development which seems to be entirely insular. The Yorkshire iron mirrors may be compared with some from Celtic lands abroad, but the Continent has nothing to match the decorated bronze mirrors. In some of the symmetry, as on the Desborough mirror [62], Roman influence may be suspected, but other designs are far removed from classical taste. Such is Old Warden [61e], with an overall network of trumpet voids (see p. 34), and Great Chesterford [61f], which Jope describes so vividly that we are obliged for ever to see it through his eyes: 'an unsteady lurch and a leering face, with wicked eyes running straight out into blunt-pointed ears, and spidery arms like tentacles wandering crazily through the available space to end in keeled-volute derivatives that look like ghoulish suckers'. One wonders how the British craftsman would have described his design, and which way up he would have viewed it, if that mattered to him.

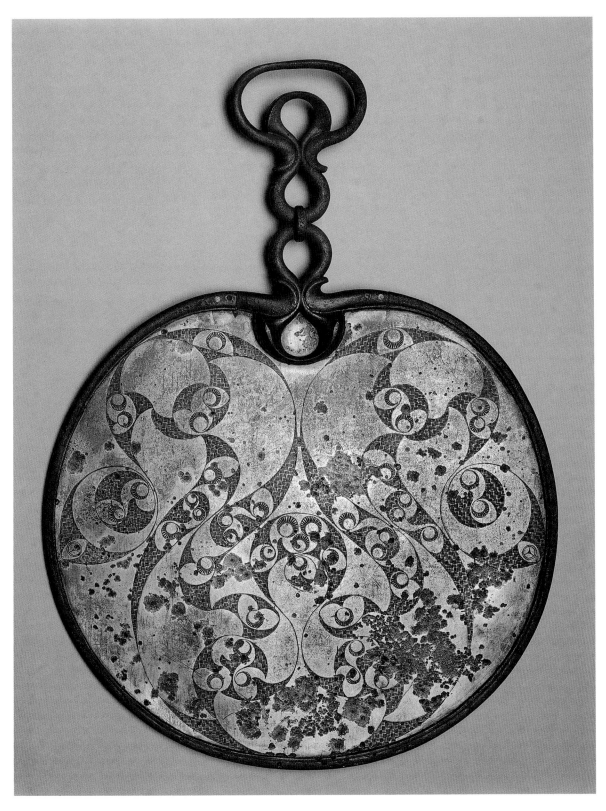

## Chapter Five | Weapons and armour

*T*HE *WHOLE RACE, which is now called Gallic or Galatic, is madly fond of war, high-spirited and quick to battle...* (Strabo)

Celtic warriors were armed with spears and swords, wore helmets and defended themselves with shields. Reconstruction drawings are well known, and usually such warriors wear the unique Thames helmet and carry the one and only Battersea shield. In order to establish the warrior's equipment, and to see how it varied from man to man, time to time and place to place, archaeologists rely on representations, historical accounts and collections of grave-goods, but for Britain information on all these scores is sadly defective.

On the Continent in the Late Hallstatt period and at the beginning of La Tène I it seems that the spear was the most popular weapon, sometimes accompanied by a dagger or short sword. The long sword was introduced in La Tène I, and by La Tène II warriors were equipped with a single spear or lance, a long sword and a shield. In Britain there are only a few burials of armed warriors so it is impossible to generalise about changes in equipment. A grave excavated at Owslebury (Hants) included the trio of spear, sword and shield, a much disturbed grave at Great Brackstead (Essex) had two spears, sword and shield, and a warrior burial at North Grimston (North Yorks) had two swords and a shield. Otherwise the only associations of weapons is the sword and spear from Whitcombe (Dorset), while swords were found with the remains of shields at Deal (Kent) and in four Yorkshire burials. In cremations it was sometimes the practice to make do with only a representative object, or indeed part of an object: the rich Snailwell (Cambs) burial, for instance, included an iron shield-boss which had been deliberately removed from the shield. No other weapon was found but it may well be that the boss was intended to indicate the dead man's status as a warrior. One weapon commonly used by the Britons but never found in graves is the sling: hoards of sling-stones have been excavated in several British hillforts.

Spears figure prominently in accounts of the Celts in battle, are the only weapons

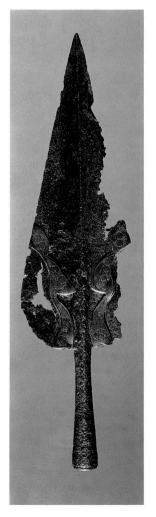

*63 Iron spearhead with bronze decoration, from the River Thames at London. Length 302 mm.*

60

mentioned in Caesar's description of his invasion of Britain, and are sometimes depicted on British coins. The remains are limited to the iron missile-head, and it is usually impossible to determine whether the weapon had been a spear or javelin to be thrown, or a lance to be thrust. Most spearheads were simply forged from iron, but very occasionally they are decorated. An iron spearhead found in the River Thames at London is quite exceptional, having a bronze openwork shape with chased decoration riveted to each side of each wing: the four shapes and their ornament are all slightly different [63]. It is hard to believe that this weapon would have been thrown at the enemy and it is more likely to have been the head of a chieftain's ceremonial spear. A curious practice involving spears has been recorded from several East Yorkshire burials. Spearheads were discovered among the bones, but they were not neatly arranged as part of the warrior's equipment. On the contrary, they had been used to 'kill' the corpse: the spears had been thrown into the grave, around and into the body, with some actually penetrating the bone.

Daggers and swords were doubtless more prestigious weapons, and were certainly more complex in construction. As on the Continent, daggers were used in Late Hallstatt times and at the very beginning of La Tène I, but in the fourth century BC their place was taken by the long sword, whose arrival presumably indicates a change in warriors' tactics. The blades themselves were undecorated, but scabbards and sheaths

64 *Dagger sheaths from the River Thames, showing a typological sequence from Late Hallstatt (left and centre) to La Tène I (right) chapes: left, Chelsea; centre, Barn Elms; right, Wandsworth. Full lengths 341, 295, and 312 mm.*

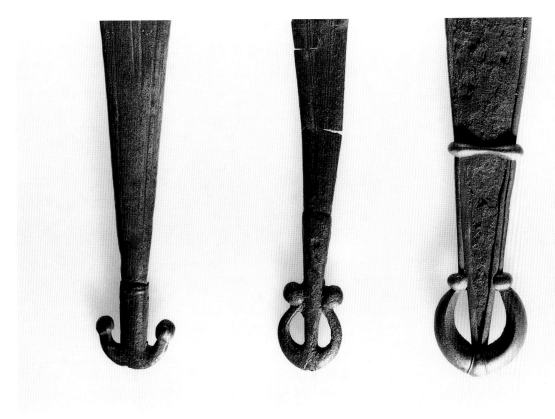

65 *Geometric decoration on the front-plate of a La Tène I bronze sheath from Richmond.*

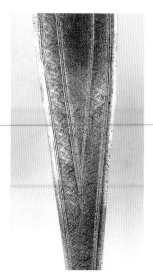

offered great scope to the artist. The earliest dagger-sheaths were made of wood, sometimes wrapped with strips of bronze and sealed at the bottom with a ferrule, but most Late Hallstatt sheaths in Britain were made entirely of metal. They have two shaped plates, a bronze front-plate (often decorated), the edges of which are wrapped round an iron back-plate, which has a suspension-loop towards the top. The tip of the two plates is secured at the bottom by a chape, which gave further scope for decoration and was subject to quite rapid typological development. At first it was tubular, terminating in an anchor-like form; then the vulnerable projecting arms of the anchor were curved back and attached to the bottom of the sheath to form an open ring-like ending [64]. The very fine cast chape from Wandsworth stands aside from this sequence, although its decoration and that of the sheath is quite in keeping with the Hallstatt tradition (see fig. 19).

When they are decorated Late Hallstatt and La Tène I sheaths have simple geometric motifs, such as lozenges, triangles and sometimes compass-drawn arcs and circles down the borders of the front-plate. The position and form of some of this ornament suggests that the inspiration came from stitching along the sides of leather sheaths [65].

Scabbards, used to house the long sword introduced in La Tène I, were often made of wood or leather, but the best surviving examples are of metal. Like the earlier sheaths, they were made of two plates, their ends clasped by a chape in the form of a frame whose top is bridged at the back and clamped at the front [66]. Few La Tène I iron scabbards are decorated, but one has chased decoration down the edges in the Late Hallstatt fashion and there are two from the Thames decorated with dragon-pairs (see fig. 27) and one from Fovant (Wilts) (see fig. 32) with a related design.

Some La Tène I blades, such as those from Standlake (see fig. 24) and the River Witham (see fig. 29), had wood or leather scabbards fitted with metal panels and chapes. The back of a bronze chape from Little Wittenham (Oxon) sports a cut-out design including trumpet voids, but the linear decoration is more reminiscent of Stage IV [67]. The scabbard found in a grave at Deal (Kent) follows this tradition, with a bronze chape and a bronze panel at the top [68]. The design executed in repoussé on the panel is essentially two interlocking S-shapes, formed by lobe and cusp motifs embellished with repoussé details very like some of the engraved fillings of Scabbard Style art. But central to the three nodes are trumpet voids typical of Stage V.

The decorated Yorkshire and Irish scabbards of the third century BC have front-plates made entirely of bronze. In Yorkshire the back-plates and chapes were iron, but in Ireland some, perhaps all, were of bronze. Three of the Yorkshire pieces were recovered complete from graves. The

66 Opposite page, left *Cast bronze La Tène I chape from Northern Ireland. Length 104 mm.*

67 Opposite page, right *Sheet bronze chape from Little Wittenham, with openwork and engraved decoration and a cast-on chape-end. Length 165 mm.*

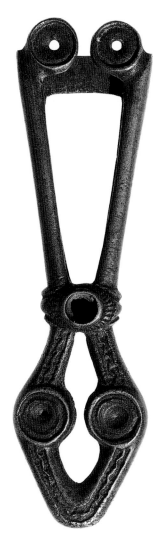

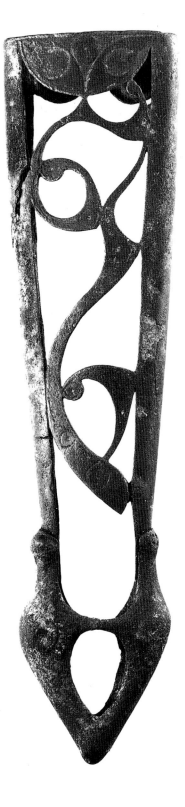

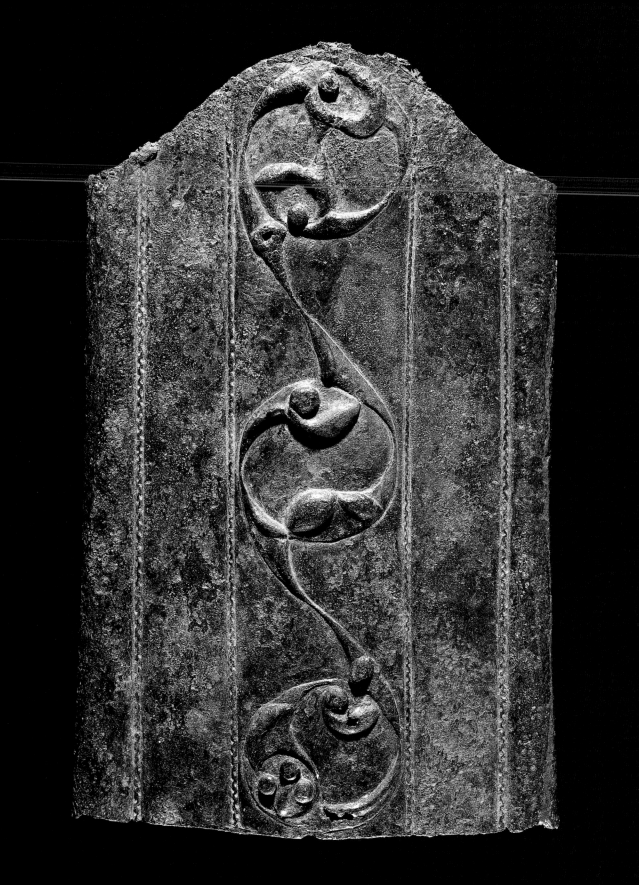

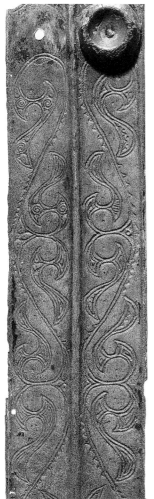

fourth, from Ferrybridge (West Yorks) is similar but fragmentary: it had been purposefully bent and broken before it was discarded, and only part of it has been recovered. Such deliberate mutilation of weapons was practised by some Continental La Tène communities, but is rarely recorded in Britain. The Yorkshire scabbard thus ritualistically killed was left in the ditch of a religious monument, which might seem very appropriate, except that the monument was Neolithic, erected some 2,000 years earlier. The six decorated Irish scabbards, too, were probably deposited in the course of religious ceremonies. Three came from the Bann, a river comparable with the Witham and second only to the Thames in terms of Iron Age artefacts. The other three were found at the end of the nineteenth century in a bog at Lisnacrogher (Co. Antrim). Over several years about seventy metal artefacts were recovered from the vincinity, and it may have been a votive deposit comparable with Llyn Cerrig Bach and indeed La Tène itself.

The overall decoration on the Yorkshire and Irish scabbards is in the form of waves or S-motifs, and one of the Lisnacrogher designs combines the two [69]. S-motifs on either side of the central ridge are paired, alternately facing and backing; in each row the S-motifs are adjacent, not linked as on the Wisbech scabbard (see fig. 23). The overall effect is of balanced waves and symmetrical tendrils, but in the filling of the upper tendrils there is no attempt at symmetry, with spirals, lobes, dots, concentric fillings and hatching all mixed together.

The La Tène I and early La Tène II scabbards held weapons with blades between 550 and 650 mm long, and the decorated Irish scabbards were for even shorter ones. But in the second and first centuries BC there was a marked increase in length, and some fine scabbards entirely of bronze were made for blades from 700 to 870 mm long. One found in 1982 at Little Wittenham (Oxon) is in excellent condition: decorated with repoussé ornament in the top panel, featuring trumpet shapes and voids, it also has fine chased 'laddering' for the length of the scabbard at either side of the central rib and cast relief ornament on the chape [70]. Related scabbards have panels of engraved or chased ornament at the top. A quite different La Tène III type is represented by the bronze scabbard found at Isleham (Cambs) in 1976 and probably from the River Lark [71]. Engraved or inscribed ornament in panels at the top and bottom of the front-plate is in near-pristine condition and the scabbard must have been

68 Opposite page *Bronze panel with repoussé ornament, from the mouth of a scabbard in a grave at Deal (see fig. 100). Length 95 mm.*

69 *Decorated bronze scabbard-plate from Lisnacrogher. Width 41 mm.*

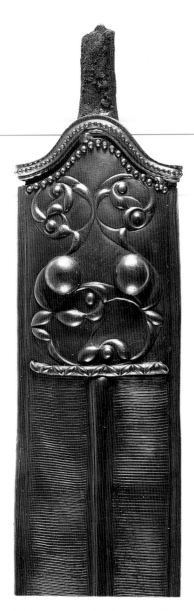

70 *Upper part of a bronze scabbard from Little Wittenham, with repoussé ornament. Width 63 mm. Photograph of a replica.*

71 Right *Bronze scabbard from Isleham, with inscribed ornament. Length 767 mm.*

nearly new when it was dropped, or thrown, into the River Lark. It has a squared instead of campanulate mouth, a rounded tip without a chape, and on the back its suspension-loop has an appendage stretching the full length of the scabbard: others of this type have been found in both the Witham and the Thames.

The Isleham sword, removed from its scabbard in the laboratory, proved to be in very poor condition, but towards the top of the blade was an armourer's mark. How far a craftsman specialised as an armourer rather than as a general blacksmith is unknown, but certainly the production of swords must have been a highly skilled branch of the trade. While some seem to have been forged from a single piece of iron, others have been constructed from several different strips and some very hard blades were achieved. Eight other British swords have armourers' marks, including one, found in the River Lark at West Row (Suffolk), little more than a mile from Isleham, which was stamped twice on one side and once on the other [72]. The West Row blade is in excellent condition: 'its suppleness is extraordinary, and it could be bent back upon itself without breaking' wrote T.C. Lethbridge in 1932 (did he try?). Lethbridge, who frequently brought dry archaeology to life, went on to speculate about the loss of the handle: 'no doubt the whole weapon flew out of the owner's hand as he was striking a blow and the unfortunate warrior was left gripping the hilt only. It is to be presumed that he did not long survive this mischance'. More mundane archaeologists would argue that the handle is likely to have perished after the sword had been discarded, because very few survive - even when the sword is still in its scabbard. Handles were usually made of wood, often in three parts (pommel, grip and guard) separated by iron washers and slotted over the tang. The most impressive is on a sword found in a decorated scabbard in a grave at Kirkburn (East Yorkshire) [73]. The pommel and guard are made of horn framed with iron inset with red 'enamel', and decorated front and back with domed 'enamelled' discs. The grip, probably made of horn too, is encased in an iron tube decorated with 'enamelled' panels.

British warriors seem to have worn little in the way of body armour. Tacitus comments that in their encounters with the Roman army they 'lacked the protection of breast-plates and helmets', but archaeology shows that iron mail was not unknown. Indeed, Varro, writing in the first century BC, implies that the Romans adopted mail from the Celts. A second grave at Kirkburn included a complete mail tunic that had been draped over the buried corpse. Made of thousands of small iron rings, each with a butt-joint and each linked to four other rings, it was found in a small group of burials unlikely to date later than the third century BC. The Kirkburn mail is as early as any from Europe, but such armour was never common: four other English sites have produced examples dating from the first centuries BC and AD. It is conceivable that most British fighting men wore nothing at all, for some of their Gallic counterparts are said to have gone naked into battle, and there are ethnographical parallels for warriors stripping to avoid being encumbered by clothes. Some British coin-types show a naked warrior, although he may represent a god or mythical ancestor.

There is evidence that Celtic warriors protected the head, but again it comes more from representations and the writings of classical authors than from archaeological remains. Several British coins seem to show warriors with leather helmets, and Diodorus Siculus records that the Gauls wore 'bronze helmets which possess large projecting figures lending the appearance of enormous stature to the wearer; in some cases horns form one piece with the helmet'. The bronze heads which serve as handle-mounts on the Aylesford bucket wear large crested helmets, those on the Baldock buckets have what seem to be leather helmets with flabby drooping horns [74], and their counterparts on the Alkham bucket have curling ram-like horns [75]. Horned helmets are shown on the Gundestrup cauldron from Denmark, and on stone reliefs from France, but this tradition is represented by only one surviving helmet in the

*72 Stamped blade of an iron sword from the River Lark at West Row. The stamp, showing a pig, has been struck once on one face of the blade and twice on the other. The X-ray photograph shows the three stamps together. Width of blade 41 mm.*

73 *The handle of a sword (length 137 mm) and the top of its decorated scabbard, from a grave at Kirkburn (East Yorks).*

74 *Opposite page Cast bronze head, a handle-mount from a bucket found at Baldock. Height 51 mm.*

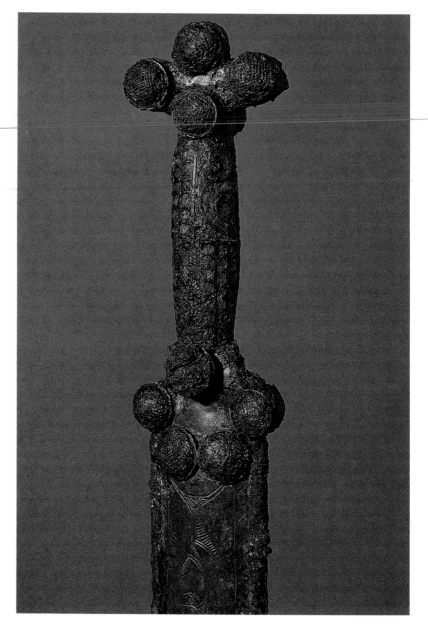

whole of Europe. Found in the River Thames near Waterloo Bridge at some time before 1866, this unique object with short conical horns was once regarded as a jester's cap [76]. It is covered with a meandering asymmetrical design whose relief-work reminded Fox of the Wandsworth round-boss and which also has an affinity with the decoration on the Torrs chamfrein, but the small repoussé lobes and shapes with hatched background are more reminiscent of the style of the Great Torque from Snettisham. It seems likely that the Thames helmet dates from the first century BC.

The only other helmet from Britain is of unknown provenance and

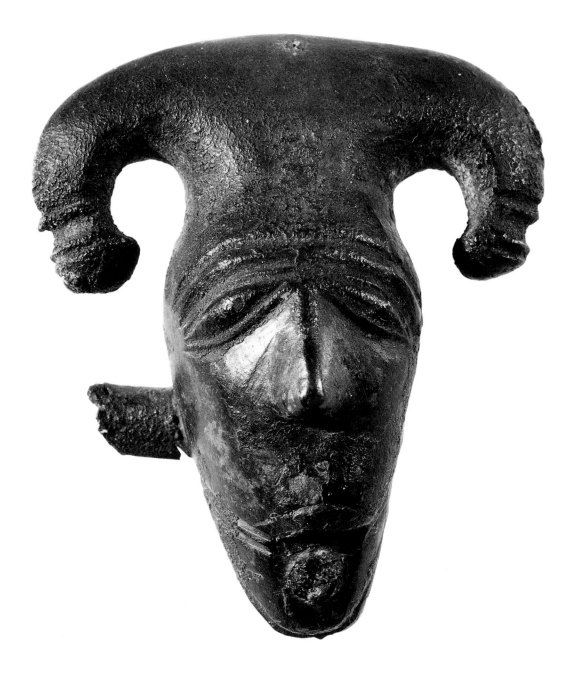

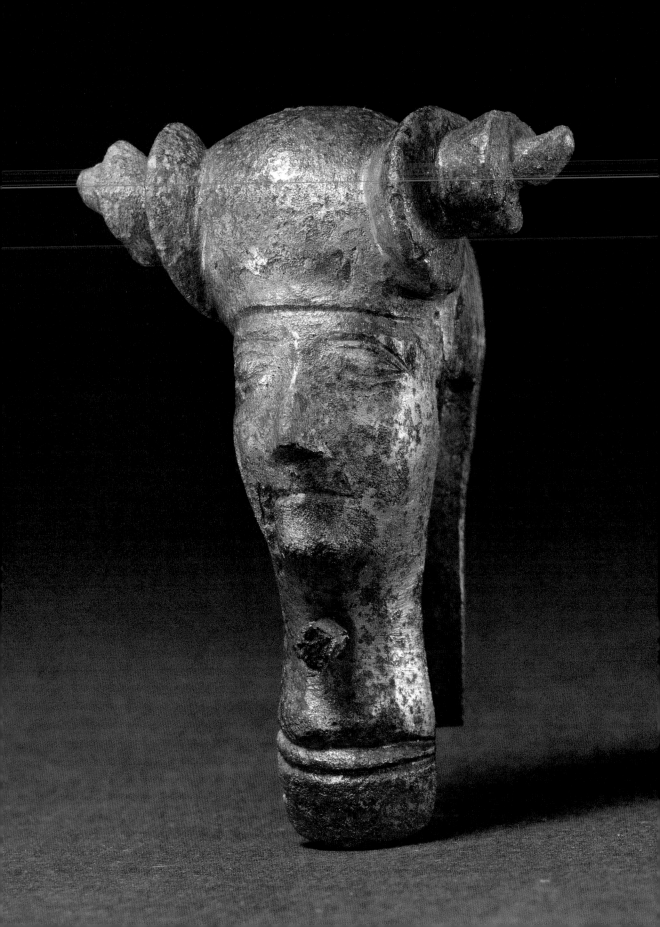

was formerly in the Meyrick Collection [77]. It too is made of bronze, but is very different in shape and decoration. Its form, a 'jockey-cap', has a long history on the Continent and the British example, whose long 'peak' (which would have been worn at the back, to protect the neck) bears a symmetrical repoussé design, probably dates from shortly after the Roman conquest.

In the absence of body armour, the Celtic warrior defended himself with a shield which was usually made of wood or leather. The typical shield, known from representations and from some waterlogged finds on the Continent, is oval in shape, with a central circular or oval hole covered on the front by a wooden spindle-shaped boss. On the back the hole is crossed horizontally by a strip of wood or iron which forms the handle, so the hand was accommodated in the central hole and protected by the boss. The only wooden Iron Age shield from the British Isles is from Clonoura (Co. Tipperary): covered in leather, it is rectangular with rounded corners, unlike the typical Celtic shield. However, there is a shield of the classic La Tène I shape from Chertsey (Surrey), found in an old watercourse of the River Thames and made not of organic materials but entirely of bronze, the only bronze La Tène shield from Europe [78]. The Chertsey shield was discovered in 1985 by the driver of a drag-line,

75 Opposite page *Cast bronze head, a handle-mount from a bucket found at Alkham. Height 44 mm.*

76 *Bronze helmet, found in the River Thames near Waterloo Bridge. Height 242 mm.*

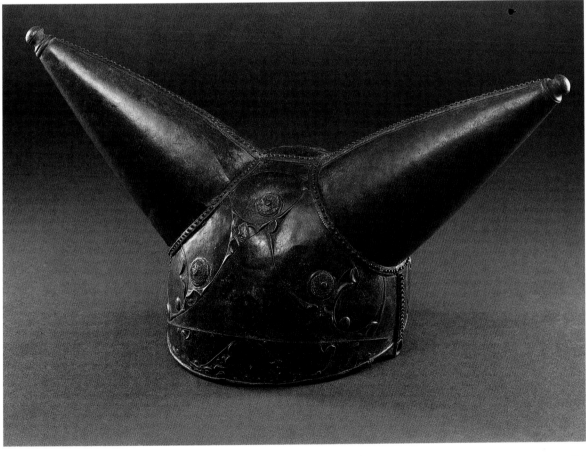

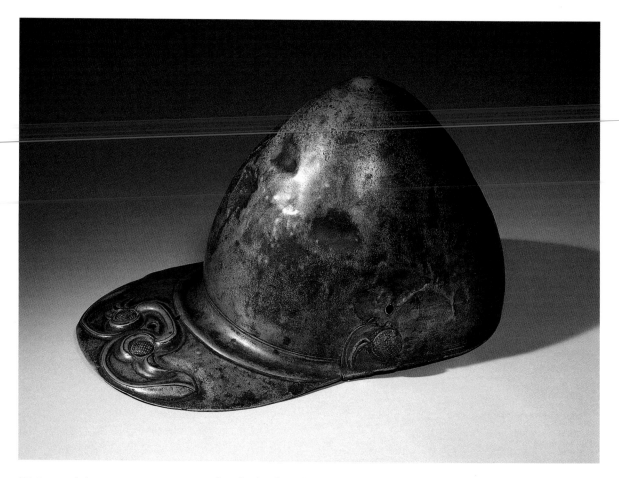

77 *Bronze helmet, provenance unknown. Height 165 mm.*

78 Opposite page *The back of the bronze Chertsey shield, showing the handle across the cavity under the boss. Length 836 mm.*

who dredged it from a waterlogged gravel pit and then successfully searched for its missing handle. This unique bronze shield is more likely to have been made for display or votive purposes than for use in battle, and the same explanation may account for the two complete bronze-faced shields also found in English rivers, and also unmatched elsewhere in Europe, the Witham shield and the Battersea shield.

The shield found in the River Witham near Washingborough (Lincs) about 1826 has the boss, spine and two terminal roundels covered by a single piece of bronze while the rest of the face of the shield is constructed from two sheets (see fig. 3). The boss itself, which is slightly above the centre-line of the shield, is exceptionally wide. Its repoussé design springs from the spine, is symmetrical across a diagonal line and seems to be based on a palmette motif. At the centre is a roundel holding three oval knobs of deep-coloured coral with two similar pieces, but circular, at either side (see fig. 16). Each terminal roundel had a central petalled boss (only one survives) ringed by an engraved scroll featuring the half-palmette, and supported by what looks like the head of a fantastic animal with large close-set eyes, petalled ears, and an engraved palmette on a snout [79]. This magnificent shield has been still further decorated across its full width with what seems to have been a boar with

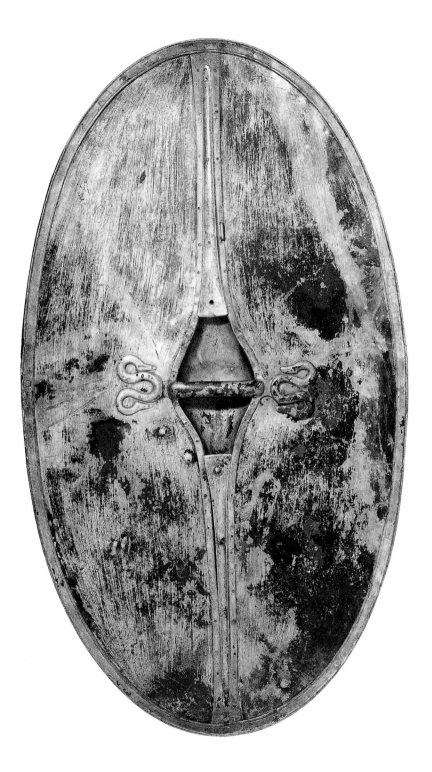

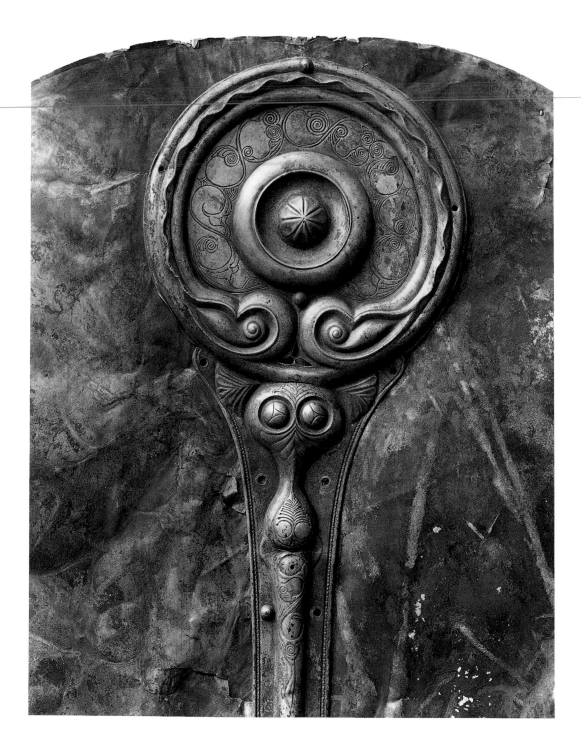

incredibly spindly legs. Only the outline of the creature and the rivet-holes which were once used to attach it can be distinguished (see fig. 3).

A very similar shield is represented by a bronze boss found in the Thames at Wandsworth: it too may have been entirely faced with bronze, but only the boss survives [81]. Much shorter than the corresponding piece on the Witham shield it differs in having had separate terminal roundels. The one surviving end of the spine-cover expands to a mask from which it takes its name, the Wandsworth mask boss, and this would have supported the roundel as on the Witham shield. The arrangement of decoration, too, resembles that on the Witham shield, in that it springs from the spine and is diagonally balanced, but the repoussé here is in higher relief and recalls some of the cast 'Plastic Style' works on the Continent. There is only a little engraving, featuring typical Stage IV tightly coiled spirals.

It may be that another form of shield is represented by a circular bronze boss also found in the Thames at Wandsworth [80]. The Wandsworth round-boss has engraving distinctive of Stage IV, much of it in the form of disjointed fragments occupying voids within a repoussé design. It has a central dished hemisphere whose broad decorated flange is roughly finished at the edge and was obviously intended to be covered by another sheet (or sheets) of bronze. The shield could have been circular, but a circular boss does not necessarily imply a circular shield, and the closest parallel for the Wandsworth round-boss is on a long shield -

79 Opposite page *Detail of the decoration on the Witham shield (see fig. 3).*

80 Below left *Bronze round-boss from the River Thames at Wandsworth. Diameter 330 mm.*

81 Below right *The bronze mask boss from the River Thames at Wandsworth (broken at the bottom end). Length 370 mm.*

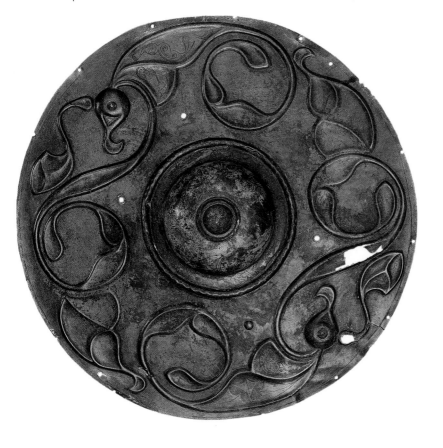

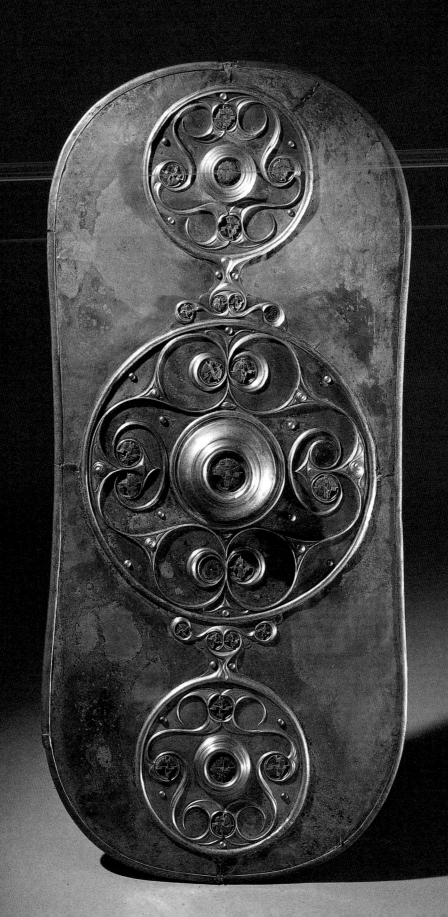

the most famous of all British Iron Age antiquities, the Battersea shield.

Like the Witham shield, the Battersea shield is in fact the bronze face and binding of a shield probably made of wood [82]. Despite their markedly different bosses the two shields are in some way related, for both have circular terminal panels which are linked to the central element by features which remind us of animal heads. On the Witham shield, and the Wandsworth mask boss, these heads face inwards because they are supporting broad roundels and narrowing through the snout to the spine of the shield; but on the Battersea shield the position is reversed - the broader element is at the centre and the animals face outwards. These Battersea animals have wide spreading antlers, and are made in one piece with the terminal roundels but quite separately from the central boss. The three panels, all with highly accomplished, steeply profiled repoussé decoration, form the central part of a shield whose background is filled with four shaped bronze sheets, each occupying a quadrant, attached by rivets that pass through panel, sheet bronze and then the underlying wood. The repoussé design on the central panel is based on an enclosed palmette which gives rise to triangular shapes on either side. Strands from the other two corners of the triangles then meet to form a circle. This motif occupies one half of the panel and is almost mirrored by the design in the other half; almost mirrored, but not quite, because there are slight differences in some of the infillings. The end panels carry similar but not exactly identical designs based on interlocking S-motifs. Prominent on both end and central panels are a series of roundels built from cast bronze frames into which a soft and malleable red glass, or 'enamel', has been pressed from the underside.

All the shields mentioned hitherto are oval with rounded ends, but a shield of very different shape was popular in the second and first centuries BC. It was equally long, but in-curved at the ends, so that it had pointed corners and resembled the shape of a hide. Fragments from the bindings of the distinctive corners of these shields have been known for many years, but their correct identification was a mystery until a collection of bronze miniature shields appeared on the antiquities market in 1988 [83]. Research showed that they had belonged to a huge collection of Bronze Age and Iron Age antiquities found a few years previously in a hoard near Salisbury (Wilts). Miniatures were often made for votive reasons, to represent the full-size originals at temples; they are faithful copies, and in the case of the Salisbury shields they even have tiny handles riveted across the space behind the boss. The face of the finest of them is partitioned into eight compartments, alternately decorated and plain. Doubtless this engraved ornament accurately represents the decoration that would have been painted on the wooden or leather original, for shields 'were decorated in individual fashion' according to Diodorus Siculus. Within months of the appearance of the Salisbury shields the remains of a full-size hide-shaped shield, 1.19 m long, was found in a grave at Deal (Kent). Its organic parts had rotted, but its shape was preserved by the bronze binding, and there were fragments from decorative bronze panels, including a piece with openwork ornament that had covered part of the boss (see fig. 35).

82 Opposite *The Battersea shield. Length 777 mm.*

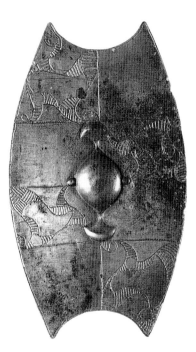

83 *Bronze miniature shield from the Salisbury hoard. Length 77 mm.*

## Chapter Six | Chariots and harness

*F*OR *THEIR JOURNEYS and in battle they use two-horse chariots, the chariot carrying both charioteer and chieftain. When they meet with cavalry in the battle they cast their javelins at the enemy and then descending from the chariot join battle with their swords.* (Diodorus Siculus)

The account by Diodorus Siculus refers to Gaul, where the war-chariot became obsolete by the time of the Gallic Wars, but when Caesar invaded Britain he found chariots used in the same way, and more than a century later some tribes in northern Britain were still employing them to resist Agricola. Some idea of the large number of chariots in Britain is given by Caesar's claim that after the British king Cassivellaunus had disbanded most of his troops 'he retained only some four thousand charioteers, with whom he watched our line of march'.

It may be that the Britons used the same vehicle for journeys and

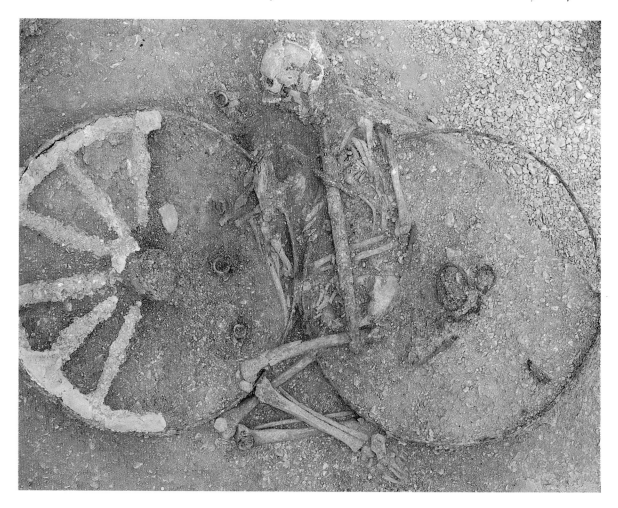

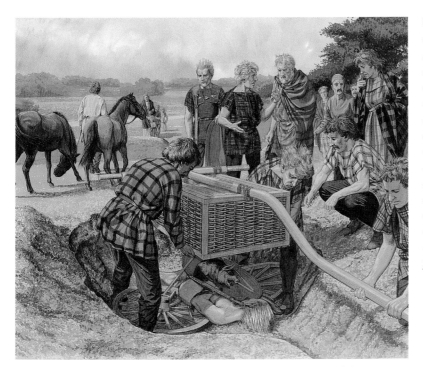

84 Opposite page *A cart-burial, one of three excavated at Wetwang Slack in 1984. The skeleton rests on top of the wheels and is accompanied by an iron sword in a bronze and iron scabbard (see fig. 30) and seven spearheads that had been thrown around and into the body (see p. 62). Within the wheel on the right are two iron horse-bits; and on the left a line of five bronze and iron terrets marks the position of the yoke. The wood of the wheel on the left had rotted to leave cavities in the soil. The excavators pumped polyurethane foam into the cavities and recovered the shape of the felloe and spokes.*

for war, but the archaeological evidence is slight and not very helpful. One day a complete chariot may be found in a waterlogged context; in 1968 a complete wooden wheel was found below the water-table at Holme Pierrepont (Notts), and the excavator did wonder if more of the vehicle was there, but circumstances prevented complete excavation. For the moment models and drawings must be constructed from scant details.

Vehicles were occasionally buried in graves in eastern Yorkshire, but soil conditions preclude the preservation of wood, so only the metal fittings have been found. In two burials near Pickering (North Yorks) carts had been buried complete: both were found with wheels upright and the clear line of a central pole could be traced in the sand of one of the barrows. Sadly those graves were excavated a long time ago, so they did not provide the amount of information that would have been recovered today. Between 1984 and 1987 five cart-burials were excavated in the adjoining parishes of Wetwang, Garton and Kirkburn (East Yorks), but there the carts had been dismantled before burial, which was the more usual practice in Yorkshire. In four of the burials the wheels had been set side by side, flat on the floor of the grave, and the corpse had been placed on top of them [84]. Alongside each skeleton a line of terrets (rein-rings) indicated where the yoke had been buried: in all the graves it had been placed on the same side of the corpse, obviously in accordance with some carefully preserved ritual. But the wood of the yoke had disappeared without trace, and the other woodwork had been reduced to mere soil-marks or the occasional cavity. The fifth grave, at Garton Station, was slightly different: the wheels had been leant against the wall of the grave, and indications of woodwork were clearer. The wooden parts of this vehi-

*85 An artist's impression of the ceremony at a Yorkshire cart-burial. It is more likely that the T-shaped frame of axle and pole was detached and placed over the corpse before the bodywork was inverted to form a canopy.*

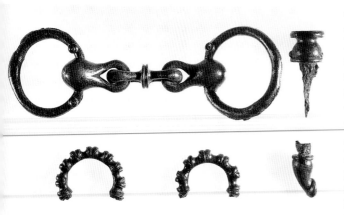

86 *Bronze and iron harness from the King's Barrow, Arras: a three-link horse-bit with cast bronze links and rings of iron encased in bronze; a linch-pin whose iron shank has corroded and broken, but the cast-on bronze terminals survive in good condition; and two terrets - the cast-on bronze is well preserved, but the iron bars have corroded and almost disappeared. The horse-bit is 272 mm long.*

87 *A set of bronze harness from Polden Hills: five terrets and two two-link horse-bits. The horse-bits are 220 and 223 mm long.*

cle had rotted leaving cavities in the compact filling of the grave. It had then been temporarily waterlogged, and clay was washed into the cavities. Thus on excavation, areas of clay were found where some of the wood had been buried, and the positions of felloes, spokes and hubs of the wheels could be distinguished, as well as parts of the pole and axle of the cart. But in the centre the filling had been less compact and of the body of the cart only a rectangular outline could be seen. It seems that the standard practice was to remove the T-shaped frame (pole and axle) and lower it into the grave after the wheels, followed by the bodywork of the vehicle which was inverted to form a canopy over the corpse [85]. The precise details of that bodywork remain a mystery.

The vehicle in the Yorkshire graves, with two wheels and a central pole, would have been drawn by a pair of horses. In the so-called King's Barrow at Arras both horses had been buried as well: one was a surprisingly old animal, of no more use in this life, and its burial is consistent with the discovery of a defective horse-bit in the same grave [86]. Two of the human skeletons in the Yorkshire graves were accompanied by swords, and one had been buried with a mail tunic, so it might be supposed that the two-wheeled vehicle had been a war-chariot. But eleven other vehicle-burials in the area had neither weapons nor armour, and two had skeletons identified as female and accompanied by iron mirrors. The vehicle is best regarded as an all-purpose cart, which perhaps also served as a hearse, and it may have been placed in the grave to indicate the status of the deceased or perhaps to speed his journey to the other world. There was no point in wasting serviceable material on this symbolic journey, hence the worn-out nag and useless horse-bit in the King's Barrow.

Iron Age and Roman wheels were made to two different patterns, with either a composite or a one-piece felloe (the felloe is the wooden

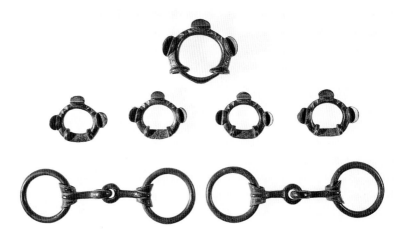

circumference bound by the iron tyre). The Holme Pierrepont wheel is in excellent condition, and was associated with a dug-out canoe whose wood has been dated by radiocarbon analysis to about the time of the Yorkshire burials. The felloe of the wheel is composed of six segments dowelled together, and each segment takes two spokes: this method of construction, which has remained unchanged to the present day, requires an iron tyre to be heated and then shrunk onto the wheel to clamp all the components tightly together. The wheel has an ash felloe with oak dowels, oak spokes and a birch nave (or hub): a modern wheelwright would choose the same woods for felloe and spokes but he would use elm for the nave. But the very little surviving evidence from the Yorkshire graves suggests that some of their wheels were made by the other method, in which the felloe was made of a single piece of ash bent to form a hoop.

The wheel was secured to the axle by a linch-pin which may sometimes have been hardwood and on one occasion at least was antler, but the best-known examples are made of metal (see fig. 12). The simplest form has bent shank and ring-head forged from a single piece of iron, but there are two other types whose straight iron shanks have bronze terminals. The one has a moulded head, flat on top or capped by a ring: sometimes both the top of the head and the end of the foot are decorated, either in relief or with enamel, and several examples are markedly worn because they have rubbed against the nave. The second type of iron and bronze linch-pin has a crescent-shaped head which provided an ideal field for enamel ornament [88].

Horse-bits made of iron, bronze or a combination of the two are found both in pairs in the Yorkshire graves and in hoards. There are two main designs, one with two links between the rings and the other with three; a prototype of the three-link bit comes from a French burial dated c. 400 BC but in Britain the type was still in use in the first century BC. The two horses would have been harnessed one at each side of the central pole, linked by a wooden yoke (the padded horse-collar was a much later development). It seems likely that four terrets (rein-rings) were strapped to the yoke, spaced equidistantly so that the reins of each horse passed through two rings. British Iron Age terrets were D-shaped, cast in bronze or with a straight iron bar onto which a decorative arc of bronze had been cast. But they occur in sets of five, not four, and the fifth terret is always larger than the others and has a broad 'saddle-shaped' bar; it must have occupied a central position, somewhere on the line of the cart-pole, and it may

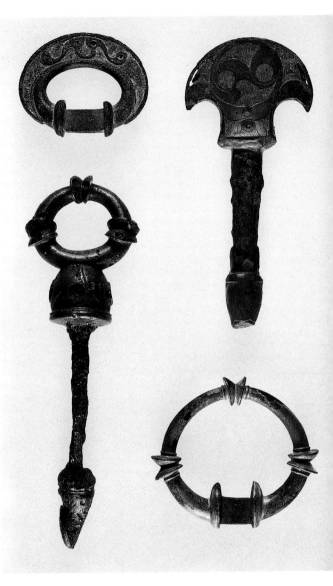

88 *Iron and bronze linch-pins from Kings Langley (above) and Stanwick (below); and bronze terrets from Westhall (above) and Stanwick (below). The linch-pin and terret at the top have been decorated with champlevé enamel. The Kings Langley linch-pin is 132 mm long.*

have helped to secure the strapping attaching the yoke to the pole [87].

The finds from pit 209 at Gussage All Saints (see fig. 10) suggest that horse-bits, terrets and linch-pins were all manufactured by the same craftsman at the same time, so they were probably acquired in full sets. One such set is seen in the King's Barrow where an undecorated three-link horse-bit is associated with a knobbed terret and a linch-pin with cast bronze head and foot [86]. The products of the Gussage smithy are more elaborate, because some of the side-links of the bits have lobed ornament in relief, the heads of linch-pins are similarly decorated, and no fewer than fourteen quite different types of terret were made. The Polden Hills (Somerset) hoard, dating from the middle of the first century AD has matching two-link horse-bits and terrets, but no linch-pins, whereas the Stanwick (North Yorks) hoard has sets of bits, terrets and linchpins. Some of the Stanwick linch-pins were surmounted by shaped rings which closely resemble the terrets [88]. A third type, contemporary with Polden Hills and Stanwick, is represented at Westhall (Suffolk) where several enamelled terrets were found. The deep decorative arc of the terret provided an ideal field for champlevé enamel, and there are matching linch-pins with enamelled heads though not found in the same hoard. Horse-bits are occasionally enamelled, but the fields available for ornament are much smaller than those on terrets and linch-pins [89]. Although buckles do not seem to have been used, harness straps must have been fastened and linked in a variety of ways and there is a wide range of strap-links and ornamental fittings, especially from contexts in the first century AD [90].

One unique piece of horse equipment remains to be discussed. Found in a peat bog, possibly once a loch, at Torrs (Dumfries and Galloway), this remarkable antiquity once belonged to Sir Walter Scott and is now one of the treasures in the National Museum of Antiquities at Edinburgh [91]. It used to be regarded as a chamfrein, the piece of armour that covered the frontal of a horse, but detailed study by Stuart Piggott and Richard Atkinson showed that it was more complex than

*89 Bronze horse-bit, with 'enamel' ornament, from Rise (East Yorks). This variety was derived from the three-link horse-bit (cf. fig. 86), but here the side-links are cast in one piece with the rein-rings.*

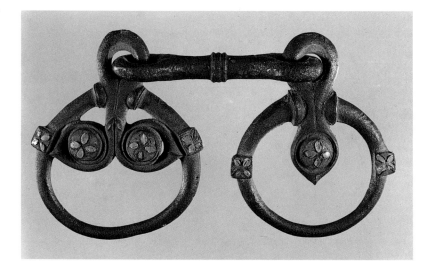

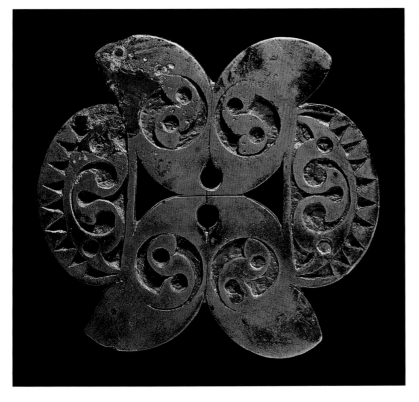

had been supposed. It seems that the horns, though approximately contemporary with the head-piece, were attached to it in relatively recent times, but before 1829 when it was first illustrated. The headpiece itself is made from two sheets of bronze decorated with fine, more or less symmetrical repoussé which respects two perforations at the sides and perhaps the damaged remains of another in the centre. There are three engraved repair patches, each disguising a crack in the sheet bronze. Experiments have shown that the headpiece is too small to have been a chamfrein, but it could have been used as a pony-cap: thus the two perforations would be for the ears and not for the eyes, and the conjectural central hole could have taken a plume. The two horns are a pair, though only one retains its cast bird-head terminal. They are decorated with different engraved designs, the motifs and fillings of which may be compared with those on the Witham scabbard (see fig. 29), Wandsworth round-boss (see fig. 80) and some of the Irish scabbards (see figs 30 and 69). The original function of the horns is obscure: they could have belonged to a horned helmet or have been the terminals of a yoke, but a more attractive notion is that they were mounts for a pair of drinking horns.

Models of British chariots are often shown with a pair of cast bronze handholds at the back, the type represented by the 'horn-cap' from Brentford (see fig. 25), but the identification of these objects is only guesswork because none has been found in a context exclusively linked with harness or vehicle fittings. They must have been attached to

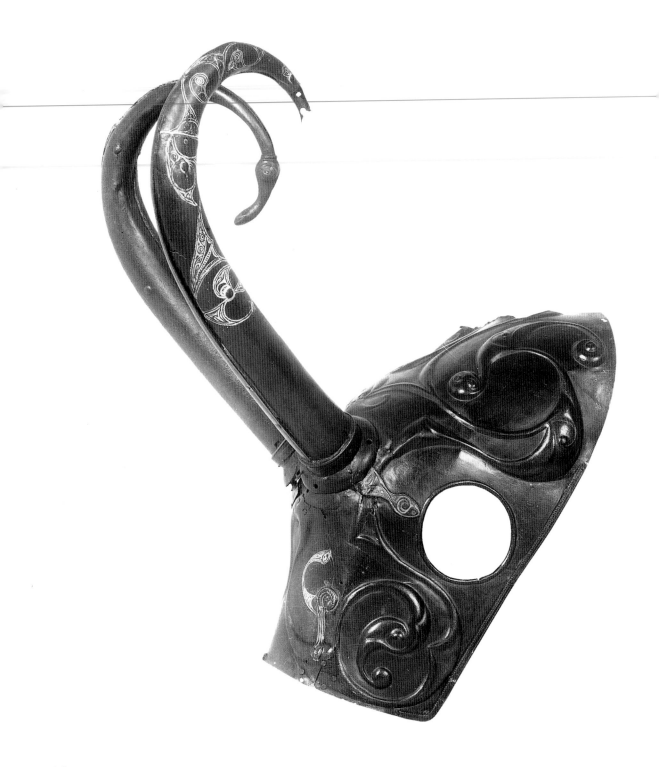

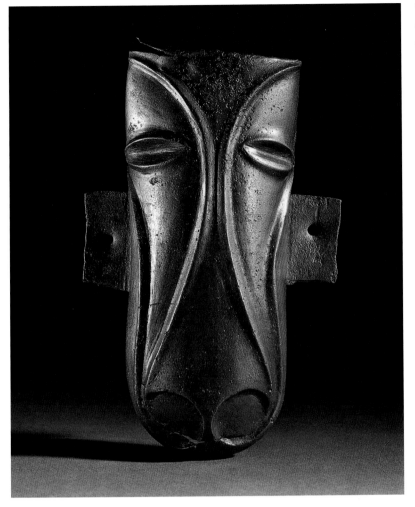

a wooden stem and the simplest explanation is that they were mace-heads. It may be that some carts had metal plaques to decorate the wood-work and it is tempting to see some of the Stanwick bronzes in this light. The doleful-looking horse-head whose face is created from abstract trumpet-motifs seems an ideal candidate for a chariot ornament, perhaps bordered by a pair of face-masks in similar style [92].

   Most reconstructions show Celtic chariots open at the front, partly because Caesar refers to the British charioteer running up and down the pole and partly because skeletons in some French graves are fully outstretched on the chassis, which would be impossible if the vehicle had a front. But charioteers would have had no difficulty in springing over a low frame, and the much earlier French vehicles could well have been modified in order to carry the corpse to the grave. Gallic coins show chariots with a pair of rounded frames side by side and a similar vehicle is represented on a stone carving in north Italy. One British coin-type shows a chariot but only two specimens of the coin are known and neither is in good condition.

*92 Bronze horse-mask from Stanwick (North Yorks). Height 101 mm.*

*Chapter Seven* | # Ritual

*A GROVE THERE WAS, untouched by men's hands from ancient times, whose interlacing boughs enclosed a space of darkness and cold shade, and banished the sunlight from above ... gods were worshipped there with savage rites, the altars were heaped with hideous offerings, and every tree was sprinkled with human gore .... The images of the gods, grim and rude, were uncouth blocks, formed of felled tree trunks .... The people never resorted thither to worship at close quarters, but left the place to the gods.*

(Lucan - a Roman poet, writing about a sacred grove destroyed by Caesar in Gaul)

Ritual is of the greatest importance to the study of Celtic art: most of the objects illustrated in this book were probably deposited in accordance with some ritual, and the designs which here are coldly classified and ordered could have been full of symbolic meaning to the original beholders. The Romans tried to understand Celtic religion in their own terms: 'of the gods they most of all worship Mercury', noted Caesar. He also distinguished two 'classes of men of some dignity and importance' - the knights and the druids. 'The druids are concerned with the worship of the gods, look after public and private sacrifice, and expound religious matters'. Druids were also philosophers and teachers, but their activities were deliberately shrouded in secrecy and their teachings and traditions were transmitted orally and never committed to writing.

In Britain places of worship certainly included sacred woods, like that described by Lucan in Gaul. Tacitus tells how a Roman governor, Paulinus, desecrated druidic sites in Mona (Anglesey): 'the groves devoted to Mona's barbarous superstitions he demolished. For it was their religion to drench their altars in the blood of prisoners and consult their gods by means of human entrails'. At the same time in the eastern part of Britain Boudicca's troops were celebrating their rebellion with 'sacrifices, banquets and wanton behaviour, not only in all their other sacred places, but particularly in the grove of Andate' (Dio Cassius). Sacred groves might well leave very little trace for the archaeologist, and none has been identified. But the Britons also worshipped in temples such as Hayling Island (Hants) where a wooden building was superseded by a Roman temple built of stone. It may be that other Roman temples had Iron Age antecedents. As for the blood and human entrails, archaeology may have a contribution to make. In 1984 workers at a peat bog at Lindow Moss (Cheshire) discovered a human body, well preserved until it was sliced by the peat-cutting machinery. Lindow Man had been killed in the middle of the first century AD: he had been stunned, garrotted, and then his throat was cut and he was bled. In his stomach there was a little mistletoe pollen (a rare archaeological find), and of course Pliny records that the druids 'hold nothing more sacred than the mistletoe'. Coincidence, perhaps, but archaeology is unlikely to find a better candidate for a druidic victim.

Crudely carved wooden gods reminiscent of Lucan's description have been found at the sites of springs in Gaul, but with one exception dated wooden figures from the British Isles are earlier than the La Tène period. More relevant, perhaps, are some small chalk carvings found in East Yorkshire that seem to date to the first centuries BC and AD [93]. Complete examples range in height from 70 to 170 mm and most are flattish almost triangular blocks of carved chalk, depicting a figure whose feet are concealed by a skirt or full-length belted cloak. Heads and arms are distinguished, and often a sword is suspended on the back. One of the carvings depicts not a figure but a shield, and two others were found in the same layer as a miniature bronze shield. Perhaps like the shields they had a religious function and represent warrior gods, mythical figures, or ancestors.

Hundreds of crude 'Celtic' stone heads are known from Britain, but not one has an Iron Age context and all must be regarded critically;

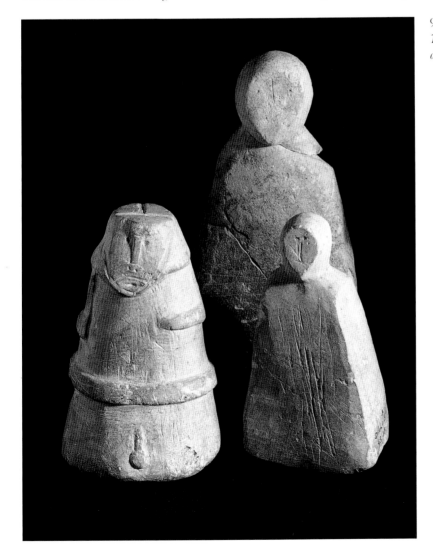

93 *Three chalk figurines from East Yorkshire. Height of the figurine on the left 110 mm.*

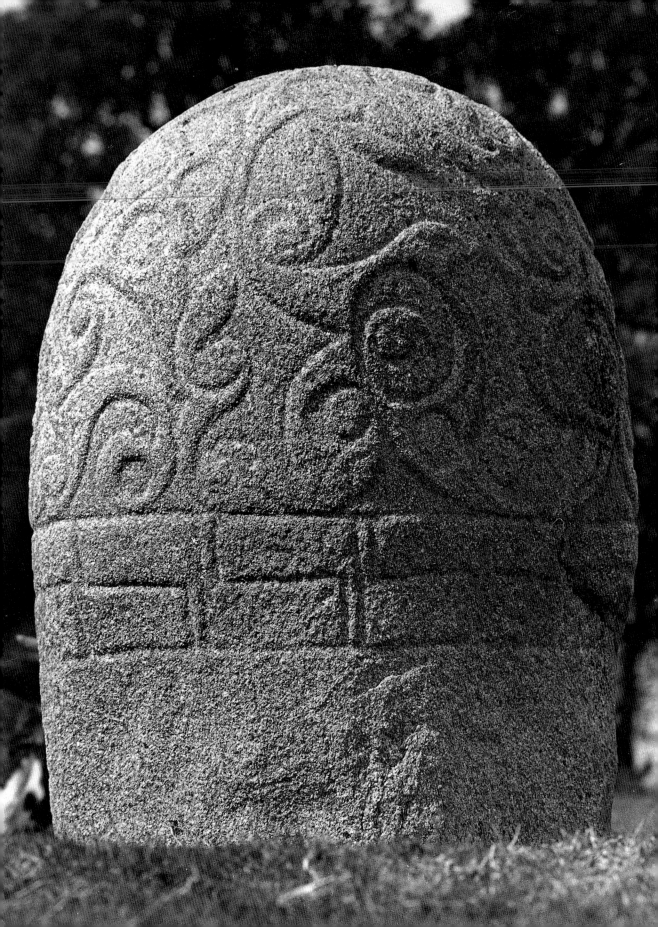

one that was accepted by most scholars has now been identified as Romanesque! Massive carved stones provide surer ground, definitely Celtic and surely ritual. There are five, all in Ireland, of which the most famous is the Turoe stone, a granite erratic covered with carvings of elaborate tendrils [94].

Posidonius, quoted by Strabo, tells of treasure found by the Romans at Toulouse: 'part of it being laid up in the temple-enclosures and part in the sacred lakes ... the lakes in particular provided inviolability for their treasures'. The type-site at La Tène was interpreted by de Navarro as 'a place where votive offerings were thrown into the water' and Fox used the same explanation for the metalwork from Llyn Cerrig Bach in Anglesey. To these examples might be added the artefacts recovered from certain rivers - especially the weapons and armour from the Witham and the Thames. Rivers are natural boundaries, and river-crossings could also be battle-sites; once a weapon has been dropped in deep water in the course of a battle its owner (even if he was lucky enough to survive) stands little chance of recovering it. On the other hand, swords which are still in their scabbards are not so likely to have been dropped by accident and the concentration of finds in selected river-beds does support a ritual explanation. It has been suggested that weapons were dropped into rivers in connection with a burial rite - perhaps in the way that Malory's King Arthur, on the point of death, instructed Sir Bedivere: 'take thou Excalibur, my good sword, and go with it to yonder water side, and when thou comest there I charge thee throw my sword in that water'. This idea is attractive in the absence of a known burial rite in much of southern England before the first century BC when cremation was introduced, but rivers have produced several swords which are contemporary with the cremation rite, and why are mirrors never found in rivers?

Ritual, too, might explain some of the figurines and a few other mysterious bronzes of the British Iron Age. A group of three bronze boar

94 Opposite page *The Turoe stone. Height above ground level c.1.2 m.*

95 *Bronze boar figurines: the three on the left are from Hounslow and the other (height 32 mm) is from Camerton.*

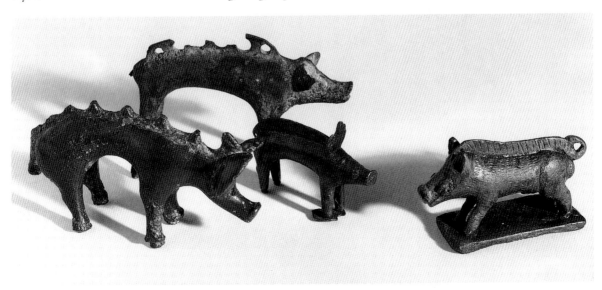

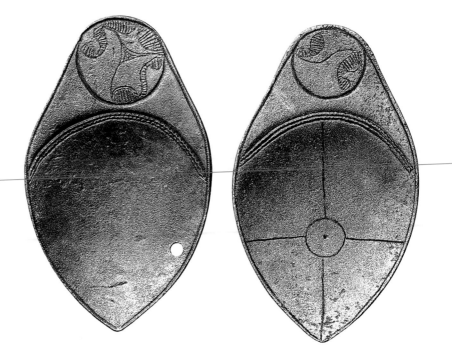

96 *A pair of bronze spoons from Crosby Ravensworth. Length 118 mm.*

97 *Bronze disc from Ireland. Diameter 280 mm.*

figures was discovered by labourers at Hounslow in 1864 along with two other figurines, possibly dogs, and a model wheel [95]. Two of the boars have high pierced crests (now broken) and the third has the remains of a stand. Perhaps they were originally on stands, like a more Roman-looking example from Camerton (Avon), which resembles a toy from a child's farmyard. Model wheels are known from votive contexts, and a boar is carved on the side of a famous representation of a Gallic god, so this small collection from Hounslow is best interpreted as ritual.

Curious spoons with short decorated handles are also likely to have had a ritual function: often found in pairs, one of which is pierced and the other marked with a cross, they are hardly likely to have been functional. Could they have been used for feeding the gods? The pair from Crosby Ravensworth (Cumbria) is typical, though with uninspired decoration on the handles [96]. They were found some seven or eight metres apart in boggy ground around a spring, 'well known for its copious supply'. As for the bronze discs from Ireland, could they have been other than ritual? Seven such discs are known, each with a circular hollow, slightly off-centre, bordered by high-relief scrolls [97].

The ultimate ritual was burial of the dead. According to Diodorus Siculus the Gauls believed 'that the souls of men are immortal, and that after a definite number of years they live a second life when the soul passes into another body'. Beliefs must have varied considerably across the Celtic world, and in Britain several different burial practices were observed. In Yorkshire the corpses were buried and then covered by small barrows raised by cutting square-plan ditches around the grave [98]. Such barrows were grouped in cemeteries but most of them have been flattened by centuries of ploughing and only recently identified by aerial photography. The Yorkshire skeletons are crouched or contracted, and some were accompanied by simple grave-goods, such as a brooch or a joint of meat.

In the rest of Britain burials are rare until the first century BC, when cremation was introduced: before that the few graves known are obviously those of a minority of the population and the normal rite has left no trace whatsoever. Most often cremations comprise only an urn to house the burnt bones, but some are more elaborate and have accessory vessels and metal grave-goods. The richest burials, in terms of the number of artefacts deposited, are centred in Hertfordshire and have large graves fully equipped with objects connected with eating and drinking. Some went to the grave with fire-dogs for the hearth and a cauldron for preparing food, and most faced the life hereafter with Dutch courage - a grave found at Welwyn Garden City in 1965 had five amphorae which together would have held more than 100 litres of Italian wine. That burial also had an Italian silver cup and no fewer than thirty pots arranged on the floor of the grave. The most spectacular item, however, was a set

98 *A La Tène cemetery in the course of excavation at Rudston (East Yorks). Centuries of cultivation have completely flattened the barrows, but below the ploughsoil the filled-in barrow ditches remain, distinctively square in plan, as well as the central graves.*

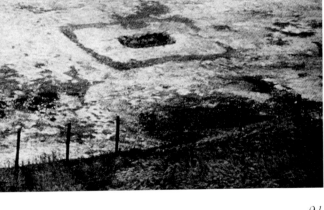

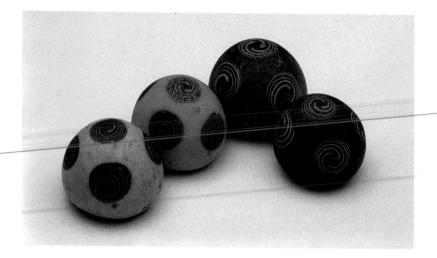

99 *Four glass game-pieces from a set of 24 found in a grave at Welwyn Garden City (see fig. 57). Height 20-22 mm.*

100 Opposite page *A skeleton found in a grave at Deal was wearing a bronze crown: here a replica of the crown is shown on the original skull.*

of unique glass game-pieces: divided by colour into four sets of six pieces, they were intended for a race-game such as ludo [99]. Grave-goods may have been deposited to indicate the status of the dead, or to provide them for a journey or with equipment needed in the afterlife. Archaeologists are left to speculate about the beliefs which have provided such an important source of artefacts.

One of the most fascinating of British Iron Age burials was found at Deal (Kent) in 1988. The skeleton was that of a man in his early thirties, of slightly feminine build, but buried with a shield, a sword, scabbard and two strap-rings, a coral-ornamented brooch and a bronze crown [100]. No other British grave has included so many pieces of Celtic art. The crown was a simple head-band of bronze with finely engraved decoration, riveted to a plain band that went over the top of the head. Too flimsy to provide protection, it must have been a status symbol, and its resemblance to Roman priestly crowns may be significant. In an earlier age such a distinguished assemblage of artefacts buried almost within sight of the Continent would have been accepted casually as the equipment of an immigrant. But every piece is distinctively British.

The Celtic art that remains for study today is not a fair sample of what was made and used by the Britons. Much of it was recovered in unenlightening circumstances, because less than a third came from archaeological excavations - and that includes nineteenth-century excavations. Nearly ninety per cent of the objects illustrated in this book were deliberately buried: about thirty-five per cent were in graves, and a similar percentage in rivers or other watery deposits, while almost twenty per cent came from hoards. Of the rest, most are isolated finds whose precise context is unknown. Metalwork is represented disproportionately because of its high rate of survival: wood, leather and even skin was probably decorated but hardly any of these materials has been preserved. However, in spite of its limitations, this selection is more than enough to show that the British contribution to Celtic art was second to none, and to establish Celtic art as one of the outstanding abstract arts in world history.

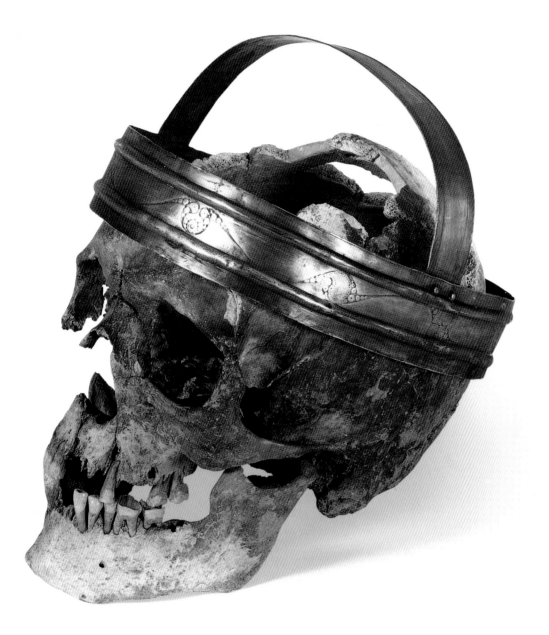

# Further reading

The present text is a reprint of *Celtic Art in Britain before the Roman Conquest* (1996), a revised version of the same title published in 1985. Through the kindness of the late Professor Martyn Jope I had already read the proofs of his standard work on the subject, *Early Celtic Art in the British Isles*, since published by Oxford University Press in 2000. Other surveys devoted to the British material alone are *Pattern and Purpose* by Sir Cyril Fox (1958) and *Early Celtic Art in Britain and Ireland* by R. and V. Megaw (1986, 1994). For the Continent, P. Jacobsthal's *Early Celtic Art* (1944, reprinted 1969) is still fundamental, while more recent volumes dealing with both British and Continental Celtic art are P.- M. Duval's *Les Celtes* (1977) and R. and V. Megaw's *Celtic Art* (1989). A full survey of artefacts in Scotland and northern England is given by M. MacGregor in *Early Celtic Art in North Britain* (1976); the Yorkshire burials are dealt with in I.M. Stead's *The Arras Culture* (1979), and there are excellent accounts of the Irish material by B. Raftery in *A Catalogue of Irish Iron Age Antiquities* (1983) and *La Tène in Ireland* (1984). A useful text book of the British Iron Age, with full bibliography, has been written by B.W. Cunliffe (*Iron Age Communities in Britain*, 3rd edn, 1991).

Coins rank among the finest examples of Celtic art and provide a wealth of information about the Britons, but they have been excluded from the present book because they bear little relationship to other art forms. For an excellent introduction see D. Allen's *An Introduction to Celtic Coins* (1978).

Books, however, are no substitute for looking at the objects themselves, and the British Musuem has an incomparable collection.

# Acknowledgements

The author and publishers are grateful for permission to reproduce the following photographs: 1. Aerofilms Ltd; 9, R.L. Wilkins; 14, 57 and 98, I.M. Stead; 18, E.M. Jope; 25, Museum of London; 36, National Museum of Wales; 42, Museum of Antiquities of the University and Society of Antiquaries of Newcastle upon Tyne; 45, Cambridge University Museum of Archaeology and Anthropology; 49, National Museum of Ireland; 67, Reading Museum; 84, A.I. Pacitto; 91, National Museums of Scotland; 94, Commissioners of Public Works in Ireland. All other photographs are copyright of the British Museum. The painting of a cart-burial, 85, is reproduced by kind permisson of Peter Connolly, and the line drawings are by Karen Hughes

# Index